Standing and Not Falling

A Sorcerous Primer in 13 Moons

Lee Morgan

Winchester, UK
Washington, USA

First published by Moon Books, 2019
Moon Books is an imprint of John Hunt Publishing Ltd., No. 3 East Street, Alresford
Hampshire SO24 9EE, UK
office1@jhpbooks.net
www.johnhuntpublishing.com
www.moon-books.net

For distributor details and how to order please visit the 'Ordering' section on our website.

ISBN: 978 1 78904 014 2
978 1 78904 015 9 (ebook)
Library of Congress Control Number: 2018931364

A CIP catalogue record for this book is available from the British Library.

Design: Stuart Davies
Photographs: Rebecca Flynn

Printed and bound by CPI Group (UK) Ltd, Croydon, CR0 4YY, UK

Standing and Not Falling

A Sorcerous Primer in 13 Moons

Contents

Thank you to Rebecca Flynn, my muse, editor, photographer, and continuous encouragement and love.

To Brett Tait, who makes everything I do possible with his practical support and by believing in me.

Thank you as well to the many direct or indirect influences upon my work that can't be named, such as Frater A, Frater B and the spirits R, A and B.

So there is no work in this world so admirable, so excellent, so wonder-full which the soul of man … cannot accomplish by its own power … Therefore the form of all Magical power is from the soul of man standing and not falling.
(Cornelius Agrippa, *Three Books of Occult Philosophy*)

Introduction

My first teacher was hardline about a lot of things. It was his belief that you couldn't practise witchcraft, or any type of occultism for that matter, if you were suffering from mental illness or addiction. Like many purists he was himself a disappointment in these arenas, because close inspection yielded the fact he was addicted to cigarettes, junk food and bossing people around. It may have been him who first drew my attention to the Agrippa quote that heads this book. After two decades in the Craft I find myself having developed a more nuanced view of what it means for the soul of man to *stand* or *fall*, and the journey I've undertaken to get here is the motivation behind this book.

When you scratch the surface of modern life it is rare to find anyone that would honestly meet with my former teacher's criterion for a suitable student of magic. Would an occultist from centuries ago like Agrippa have considered their souls to be standing in their power, or slipping into being less than themselves on account of this? Would his perspective be relevant to the pressures of today? Perhaps the uprightness metaphor is no longer meaningful or helpful today, and we can simply extract the sentiment, that we have divinity inside ourselves and it can be found through will and belief in the same.

Most people in this increasingly precarious-feeling world, even the ones who protest most vigorously, use some kind of soma or stimulant against the soporific effects of modernity, or at least struggle with depression or anxiety. Many people arrive at the door of an occult practice far from ready to learn, but more in a vein of hoping to be saved and reformed by the practice or its people. In fact, many who identify themselves as witches seem to see a close connection between their abilities and what one may term their adversary, walking a fine line between gifted and mentally unbalanced.

Some of the most Sighted, inspired and fascinating people I've met in the occult world have also been potentially the most unstable and sometimes even the most addicted. Unwilling to throw the baby out with the bathwater I have been inclined to take risks on people with all kinds of struggles, from former members of Christian cults, through to those who have been institutionalized or are heavily drug dependent. Some of these people find witchcraft acts as a panacea for all their ills, taking pent up energies that formerly went in other directions and re-purposing what they feared was mental illness in a new direction. For others this is not the case. Some have their symptoms exacerbated by magical practice and should very definitely seek concurrent help with a mental-healthcare professional, or perhaps not practise at all. Others simply continue to struggle without resolution, with occult practice seeming to neither exacerbate nor improve their condition.

Having seen examples from all of these categories I neither agree with my first teacher's take on things entirely, nor believe that witchcraft holds some kind of cure-all for the masses that can be easily converted into self-help format. Being from a Traditional Witchcraft background I am perhaps pre-disposed towards a viewpoint that the Craft is not for everyone. So where I find myself today is very much on the middle way, in this regard. I find myself not wanting to close my mind to the inspired, half-mad geniuses of the occult world (for how much less rich and interesting would our history be without them!) but not wanting my time wasted by people who come to the path purely for therapy, rather than to give themselves to magical practice as a fully realised adult ready to take responsibility for themselves and their own development.

In answer to this, what I have tried to write here is a primer of the things I wish could be covered and cleared before a student even sets out on the path, whether that setting out is solo or with a tradition that plans to guide them to initiation. I have aimed to help the new occultist stay afloat in a world where 'standing' will code for functionality and 'falling' will code for totally melting down. To this effect I have organised the information to sit beside practical activities to be carried out over thirteen moons. Ideally this would take place before the student even embarked but is useful at any stage of our development as a kind of 'detox for the soul' in these trying times, as a kind of renewal of vows when you're ready to push further, or an attempt to blow the cobwebs out of your current practice and shake things up.

This book aims to take into account some of the ills we battle against as practitioners of magic in the modern world, many we are so familiar with they become barely visible. To take aim at the biggest disconnections from ourselves that cause the leap between the uninitiated and the initiate to seem so much more traumatic than it really needs to be. For this reason these exercises are purposely constructed to be suitable for everyone, regardless of what form of witchcraft or other magical tradition they are entering. These chapters and the exercises that go with them are meant to be read and executed in order, possibly more than once over. Whatever discipline and seriousness you put into them will determine how much you get out of them. No teacher, whether an author or in-person guide, can do that work for you if you aren't prepared to take responsibility for your own progress.

Moon 1

'Belief-Belief'

> Scepticism should be dialectical. Doubt A, then doubt NOT A, then doubt both A and NOT A, then doubt your own ability to doubt enough. Doubt also Doubts itself. Experiment with Alternative belief systems, enter alternative, cognitive grids, and as the Zen Master said when asked the way of the Tao, 'Move!'
>
> (Robert Anton Wilson)

When I speak to people about belief they are quick to assure me they already *believe* in magic. Why else would they be here in the first place, trying to learn it? In fact, enquiry about where their belief levels is often met with mild offence and at the very least, resistance. Belief relates back to the fundamentals of why we practise occultism at all, it asks of us big questions about the universe and it seems to demand of us some kind of answer. Yet it can be hard to be honest with others about belief, with many claiming a certainty that may in fact be exaggerated.

I think if we have to search for why people defend themselves and over-exaggerate their belief in magic when questioned I would say this reaches back to the fact our society is still largely Christian in mindset, in ways it's only half aware of, and belief equated with faith, faith is equated with virtue. To not possess faith is to lack in virtue and the appropriate response to being told you lack virtue is shame. So to some, me asking them about their belief-levels is like questioning their virtue and state of belonging in the magic-practising community and seems like an attempt to shame them.

This is a way of thinking I believe needs shaking up considerably from the get-go. For a start, there are more shades of grey between belief and non-belief. Whilst I would agree that most people who actively seek out magical practice 'believe' in the potential for its efficacy to some degree, there are still a lot of stages of belief actualization that you watch a student pass through. You only have to witness the expression of disbelief and wonder on a person's face when they witness their first semi-miraculous happening as the result of sorcery to know that you are seeing someone whose belief has just jumped up a notch.

Most people begin with a kind of provisional belief; as they have certain experiences that begin to build, their power as a sorcerer also grows. There are a few reasons for this, which I will return to later, but for now let's just accept the connection between what I like to call 'belief-belief' (belief confirmed by experience) and increased ability to practise magic. We can experiment and prove the connection to ourselves later, for now let's have a look at what creates blocks in this process.

Overwhelmingly, the people I meet who practise witchcraft or occultism of any stamp have a far above average education level and many of them the IQ to go along with it, something that due to failings in the school system they may or may not be aware of. Higher education means being exposed to a whole intellectual universe where scepticism is embedded in the language, formed by certain half-unspoken assumptions that the writer is speaking to a sceptical, scientific atheist.

Recently I was reading *The Mind in the Cave: Consciousness and the Origins of Art* by David Lewis-Williams. I was on my way home from an international trip where I had seen rock art from the Paleolithic in person and wanted to learn more. It might have been because I was reading on the plane, and in an exhausted and vulnerable state, but part of the way through the read I began to feel a subtle yet pervasive sensation akin to a mild magical attack. It had been invisible to me during the days of my university education, being immersed as I had been in the language of scepticism. But having spent some time writing in isolation, what had been an invisible force suddenly became something I was conscious of.

I found myself feeling very aware of the author's utter assumption of cultural superiority over anyone who engages in 'magical thinking' including our ancestors and peoples around the world who still live traditionally. It was so clear that he had not gone out to find *any* possible explanation for the phenomenon he was looking at, he had gone out to find one that fitted with the leading assumptions of academia as an institution. There were certain possible conclusions that were off the table from the get-go and yet the premise that led to them was neither exposed nor explored.

In Graham Hancock's treatment of similar subject matter in *Supernatural* he puts forward a radical proposition: what if the simplest explanation for the belief in every culture around the world, prior to our own, about interaction with spirits is that people are telling the truth as they experienced it? So rather than assuming they are all mentally ill or in some way dishonest, or childishly inferior to ourselves, let's at least keep our mind open to all possibilities, with one of those possibilities being that their experiences reflect a reality of some sort. Or in other words, in some way or another, spirits exist, consciousness echoes on outside of time and not all forms of sentient life assemble bodies in the way we do.

Hancock's book didn't claim to have the *proof* that this was so, or even to personally advocate this belief, he was just open to it as a possibility. But Lewis-Williams' book also didn't contain any proof that they *don't* exist; it's just taken as assumed knowledge, a little nudge-wink between author and reader. I am well aware that from a scientific angle the burden of proof rests on the person claiming supernatural agency, not the other way around. However, the proper scientific response to any question that can't be either proven or disproven via normal means is simply a 'jury's out'.

Nonetheless, with the full power of the academia behind him, a writer like Lewis-Williams can confidently assert that cave art was the result of hallucinations, which were common to our ancestors in their primitive and non-scientific stage of development, due to bicameral mind, and are still common amongst some of our modern population. Though he admits we are physiologically identical to our Paleolithic forebears he seems to put across that consciousness has taken some leaps forward in the form of modern, scientifically, literate mankind and therefore less of us now require these mind fantasies. He makes some ironic asides about how some of us are so willfully behind, believing in voices in our heads still, even when science has supplied us with better explanations.

It wasn't just the reductiveness of his vision, or lack thereof, that gave me the sensation of being under attack, it was the realisation of how common this self-satisfied perspective is. Not a question was asked about how happy or mentally well these ancestors were by comparison to us, and what vital purpose their 'primitive' behaviours might have served for them, before we even consider their truth value. It was as though there were only two possibilities to choose between (to quote Aldous Huxley) madness and insanity. We must either accept that all magic and spirituality is poisonous superstition and side with reason, or we will succumb to a world of brutal irrationalism ruled by terrifying waves of emotionalism.

We have reason to fear the latter as well as the former; I would never deny that, as we live in an age taking a large swing towards nationalism and the associated process of voting from the feeling centre. Perhaps though it would serve us to address this without wild swinging motions between extremes? All this got me to thinking about belief in the modern era as a kind of ongoing battle against an enemy that you can't see or define, but is everywhere trying to make you forget the wonders you've seen, or write them off as something wrong with you.

I would not want for a moment to suggest there isn't any such thing as mental illness or visions that function as disruptive hallucinations, but to 'believe-believe' in magic in a modern, educated, post-industrial context is to be *at war*. It is to hold fast to your vision against a hundred voices, many of them authoritative and clever sounding, voices written with the assumption they aren't speaking to anyone who themselves sees visions on cave walls, voices that adjust their tone to patronize when they realise they are … To counter that we need to hear clever voices questioning them from positions of enquiry rather than faith. We need to see that rampant irrationalism is not the only position possible other than dry reason; there are ways to combine both perspectives into a whole and healthy human experience.

Is it any wonder, with this social backdrop that belief-belief doesn't just drop into our laps? Yet despite this assault against our magical senses, which begins when we are children and never lets up, our first instinct upon being asked about belief is shame! We are ashamed of our doubts, or our half-mast style of semi-conviction so we protest our belief the way a Christian might before a church leader. In reality this is not a moral question, certainly not an ethical matter up for interpersonal debate, it is a matter for the inside, for an environment of reverie, something so important in this modern world of performative signaling. A question to ask one's self in all seriousness and secretiveness. Not just: how much do you believe in magic? But *what do you believe magic is capable of?* What are its outer limits?

This last question is important, not just because your subconscious beliefs in this regard (whether you admit them or not) will set limits on what your magic indeed will be capable of, but because it helps in forming magical fraternity with others. If you decide to do so you will want to work with people whose perceptions of what sorcery is capable of match your own to some degree. Once a woman tried to join our coven, she believed that as a child she had been able to squash insects and then use magic to raise them from the dead. An elder I sought the advise of at the time believed this was concerning and felt the woman was delusional.

My own take on the woman's story was a little different to his, though I did not have the confidence at that time to say so. I was less interested in the objective truth-value of the story as what she had *experienced* and in what context it was true for her. Perhaps she had been experiencing the moth's Otherworldly rebirth after death and seeing the spirit as real as the squashed body? I was aware after all that I myself have witnessed things that I would swear happened to me whilst in my body interacting with other bodies, that don't seem possible to have taken place in the same reality we live our daily lives. When it comes to magic, reality is a complicated matter. And if we were to be truly scientific, wouldn't we engage in a testing sort of relationship with it, rather than trying to lock it down to one definition only and immediately accuse others of mental illness? One of our questions should always be: what effect on their life does this belief have?

The situation we find ourselves in when it comes to the mainstream 'consensus without evidence' that the spirit-world does not exist is one of historical reaction. If you understand the past four hundred years of European culture as a whole, with specific focus on the Enlightenment and what came before it, you will know that scientific thinkers and rationalists began as champions against negative superstition, as anti-witch burners who crusaded against the cruel and inhumane actions of their times. Many modern day atheists act like they are still these figures, and indeed there are those for them to react against who act like the same religious zealots of the past, so much appears frozen in time, as if these two polarities are locked in a death roll with each other.

I think that in further response to the wave of religious extremism from both extreme Christian and Muslim factions more recently that science continues to be in reaction against these same dangers. Rather than being able to consider the question without emotional bias or peer pressure, two things that greatly hamper the ability to use pure reason, most seem driven by their dislike for the excesses of their enemy rather than an objective willingness to discover truth in any form. To play into the hands of the enemy by admitting we don't really have any proof these things we scorn don't exist, and the fact that every traditional culture on earth has possessed remarkably similar ideas at the root of it all about how the spirit world functions, would be to break ranks with the good guys who gave us progressive values. Or so it seems.

So for educated people, having been immersed in that perspective to at least some degree (and maybe even used it as a tool to escape a strict religious upbringing) we need to gather some compelling evidence for ourselves as to why we should believe-believe. What I suggest students do is begin to amass a diary of the most potent supernatural or magical experiences/

successes you've experienced in life. Keep coming back to it over a series of days. Once you start thinking about it you may be surprised by how many you come up with. Try to describe them in vivid details as well as you can remember them, as sometimes the details of such experiences fade until people come to almost forget them. This is something the human mind seems predisposed to do, as if it doesn't quite know how to deal with these anomalies and softens the edges of them into gradual doubt.

To combat this forgetfulness it is best to read over and amend your list regularly. You will want to create a sense of growing conviction, an active sort of feeling, you aren't just passively accepting something you are manufacturing belief for the purposes of a grand experiment with reality. This state of proactive engagement is what I mean by 'belief-belief'. It's not blind faith; it's pursuing certain experiences with a radical openness on the topic of possibility.

We can all too easily fall back to seeing this as some typical matter of faith as discussed in religion, but if you look at it from the perspective of spirits it seems more practical than that. It seems to have more to do with being noticed. People who don't 'believe-believe' belong to a different consensus reality, which doesn't light them up the way we appear illuminated like a beacon. This is why the dead tend to make a bee-line for people with the Sight or who have recently begun to practise magic. You have hung out a beacon sign for them. It's not likes spirits are impatient of dealing with mortals who don't really believe in them, it's that they don't even seem to notice them much! The same way those non-sighted living folk don't notice them ...

This seems easy enough, but due to our mainstream world and some other factions, belief is not a one off achievement, it is something you will have to defend in yourself all your life. Not in a defensive or shrill manner, which tends to betray a certain lack of confidence, but in a quietly stubborn sort of way. You will notice that you sometimes benefit from being reminded of what you have previously achieved and that it helps to have been *recently* reminded by others of the potential effectiveness of something. Therefore the next stage in this exercise is to get together with likeminded friends, either in person or if that can't be achieved then on the internet, and share your lists with each other. Between all of you this will read as a long cacophony of magical happenings.

The reason this all matters so much before we even set foot on the path of magic is that people can see the things they expect might happen a lot better than what they expect won't. It also matters how much and how regularly that reality is supported by others. This is why a witch hundreds of years ago didn't seem to go through the same self-examination and scepticism about whether she really met a horned devil at the fence stile in the flesh or whether it was a hallucination.

Not having a word for hallucination makes it easier not to worry about hallucinations. Her culture supported, even down to the words it had and didn't have, from childhood onward, the notion that such things as manifest horned devils were possibilities. So strenuously was it believed that the practice of meeting with such individuals was against the law, meaning even the educated class of the day were firm believers in witchcraft, devils, angels and other assorted spirits. For a witch like Isobel Gowdie, there was no towering authority of any stamp that held sway in her time saying such things didn't exist, only that they were bad. And there is a far shorter leap from bad to misunderstood than there is from untrue to true! It is hard to stress enough what a radically different framing reality would have had for people in the past.

My own helpers tell me that to spirits belief-belief looks like a series of lights all coming on at once, beginning to form a big beacon fire on the hill top signalling them. Societies where the whole clan or tribe believe-believes are therefore very attractive to spirits. They will make amazing things happen (once) under such conditions, but won't continue unless fed and acknowledged. A lot of Westerners who aren't held and supported by a tradition that passes such lore to them will have some remarkable happenings at the beginning of their career, which they often struggle to get back to. One of the main reasons why is that we have no framework which tells us how to acknowledge and encourage more of the same thing to happen.

So, the conscious alteration of our immediate consensus reality can be the next level up in magic, and that's why sharing all these successes is helping you all to build more power as a collective. Each of you is having these experiences alone or with a working partner, but how often are we sharing them to help build our collective power? And henceforth, how many of these experiences happened to you together as a coven as they so often used to and in some quarters still do?

Don't worry though if your answer is that you've seen a slowdown since adulthood, or that they never happen when other people are around even though you practise with others, as this is typical of the trajectory of most covens or magical fraternities. In the beginning the extreme examples of magic happen to individuals when alone, over time they are able to build a consensus reality that this kind of thing happens, which becomes a more powerful generator of such experiences than what any of them were alone. To do that takes two things, and the first is building up a culture of regular consensus where these things are shared, supported and reaffirmed regularly.

As an aside: To know what your true state of belief-belief is you have to look at what you *do*, not what you *say* or even *think*. Action is a better measure of where you are at than what you think you think ... Due to early shaming around belief most people will report a much higher level of conviction than they really feel. We will be returning many times to the subject of shame throughout this book, as it is among the top enemies of optimal preparation for magic. Shame closes us up inside ourselves, encourages us to make ourselves smaller and tells us we are undeserving, it also makes empathy and harmonious relations with others more difficult because closing up means closing down to others' needs and feelings and often in a defensive manner that pushes away rather than draws in.

The questions to ask yourself instead are: how do I live my life? Is magic and the spirit world a major priority or does it rank pretty much below all the material 'important' stuff? Do you feel ashamed (there's that word again) when you do prioritise a magical occasion or need over a daily life need? Or do you act on your vision over everything with the willingness to entirely change your life to follow the magic? Would you take a magical emergency as seriously as a physical one? Or is there some small part of you play-acting still or treating other people's magical experiences as a type of play-acting? If you find there is it is a good thing, because you have found a way you could improve your Craft. This mindset is a good one to set from the get-go because it works against shame, whenever you discover something you can admit you are lacking in congratulate yourself! Not only have you been self-aware and courageous enough to see it, you have now also discovered a ripe space for improvement.

Here is another thing to consider:

If we've received any instruction whatsoever we will know not to go into ritual, spell work or even meditation with rigid expectations trying to force something. But there is a difference between having rigid expectations and a sense of what *might* happen. What do you go into ritual thinking *might* happen? Do you expect that some of the things listed on your night of sharing magic *might* happen to us collectively at any given moment without warning? Or do you unconsciously set the assumption (and thus the intent ...) that this ritual will be much like the last in its effectiveness and impact?

With this in mind I'd like you to attempt two things as part of this experiment:

Next time you go to do magic (anything from a spell to just sitting in a power place in nature at night) read through the list of your friend's experiences and your own successes right beforehand. If you are getting together with other occultists talk about it together. Affirm to yourself, or selves, verbally: 'These are things that happen.' Meditate beforehand on shedding the expectation that this will be just like the last time you hoped magic would happen and it didn't. Rather than thinking about when something didn't happen you could be instilling in yourself the sense of wonder/excitement/dread that 'anything may happen', up to and including a melting of the Veil between the world or the movement of objects without rational cause etc. Just because it didn't happen the last five times doesn't mean this isn't the one ... Because this isn't just optimism and positive thinking, this is creating a beacon for the spirits. Organise to unpack the topic of belief over four weeks, culminating in the experiment towards the full moon. It would be wise to make weekly diary entries about the effects of the work and to stay in the habit of doing so throughout the thirteen moons.

If you find you have time left over in this first least busy of the thirteen moons we will cover, please feel free to read ahead for the next couple of chapters. This will facilitate you being able to make preparations for the work by acquiring necessary ingredients and objects in advance, but please do not rush ahead in any of the work as it is meant to be worked through in order, and at this particular pace.

Moon 2

The Dragons are Fighting, the Tower will not stand

> Simple psychology and self-help are pale wraiths in comparison to the boons and dangers of witchcraft.
> (Peter Grey, *Apocalyptic Witchcraft*)

Many of you will be familiar with the story of Myrddin (more popularly known as Merlyn) and his connection to Dinas Emrys. In the story the tower of Vortigen would not stand, no matter how many times it was built the foundations just would not hold. The King summoned a wise man and asked for the reason. He was informed that there was a red and a white dragon at war beneath, and only the sacrificial blood of a child born with no father could stop the conflict. King Lludd is said to have charmed the dragons into a hole with silk and some bowls of honey mead. The dragons went into the silk to drink the mead, became drunk and fell asleep. These potent earth forces could then be buried and returned to the earth in a different location. This appeared to appease them.

Usually the red and white dragons have been interpreted as racial symbols standing for the red Brythonic Welsh and white encroaching Saxons, but here they will have a different mythic resonance in this book. In our current story the white dragon represents the forces of the intellect that is at war with the red animal of the body. Yet they are each so much more than this as well, for during states of war a certain distortion of the qualities of the enemy is (without some personal effort) quite inevitable.

I have begun to introduce a historical sense of the red and the white dragons fighting since the beginning of this book, even before dragons or serpents were mentioned explicitly. We have talked about them in terms of the rise of reason and its failure to fully account for or satisfy the irrational side of human nature. It is from this distorted white dragon that we must wrestle back our ability to listen to the red currents of body knowledge. The form of knowing that tells us via our clever neck hairs when we are in the presence of the sublime and the weird. Once we have done that, rather than banishing the white dragon, we must re-instate this prince of consciousness to where he belongs. Placing him in a state of harmony rather than simply reversing the roles of oppressed and oppressor. Reason and instinctual intelligence are two very different human faculties that have their place in their own contexts and need to work together if humankind is to be crowned with the full potential of consciousness. There is a time for magic and a time for science, and a time for powerful combinations of both.

Firstly, to fully understand the war going on in each of us, we must story-forth the existence of two further dragons. The dragons that aren't mentioned in the original tale are those black and glas (meaning misty-green in Welsh). These four dragons are all at war within mankind and we need a dragon tamer with mead like King Lludd to bring them into harmony. It is no accident that these are also the colours of the Four Horsemen of the Apocalypse, as like all primordial forces of life they can be a force of destruction when out of balance. In this case the mead used to charm them back into harmony is the sweet honey-wine of story. At the last moon I asked you to mount a compelling tale in favour of belief-belief, here I am going to up the ante and ask you to follow me into the realm of mytho-logic.

Mytho-logic is the love child of the white and the red dragons when they stop fighting. Whether we knew it or not we have been dealing with it in the form of stories since we were born. We've been using them actively too, questioning the story of Western rationalism and considering other stories we might want to tell about reality. Rather than fighting with the edifice of rationalism we ascribe the white dragon's wonders to its right place, such as monitoring climate science, composing symphonies and designing life-saving medicines, but we do not allow it to be a tyrant over the matters of the heart. For it does not yet speak that language, you need to teach it that and it needs to become humble enough to learn.

When I begin to explain the nature of the two subsequent dragons you may experience some temptation to ascribe them to the four elements or the four humours of a system you already work in, but please try and resist this impulse. In the story I'm telling there are four dragons, they are not elements or humours; they are dragons. Whether they are strictly real in the literal sense or not is inessential, what matters in the context of this story is that they are natural forces that self-identify as dragons.

This may seem like reinventing the wheel and that's because it is. Whilst on its own remaking the wheel sounds like hubris on the part of a younger generation of occultists wanting to set fire to history, there is far more going on here. For that would just be reversing which dragon is winning, and that will not allow the tower to stand either. What I suggest is a union of sorts between what Rudolph Steiner called the Ahrimanic and Luciferic forces, those of tradition and stability and those of innovation and freshness. On the side of Ahriman, I will say that Rudolph Steiner's *How to Know Higher Worlds: a modern path to initiation,* despite its strongly different terminologies and framework has some useful material in it for someone looking to read already extant occult primers.

We need to remember the past and absorb what it has to offer, but we also need to access new stories. Those new stories will inevitably also be old stories, upcycled into new things via alchemic recombinations and distillations. As W. H. Auden put it: 'the words of a dead man are modified in the guts of the living'. We need fresh perspective, or re-fabricated ones, from which to step back and look at both the structure of the paradigm of Western thought, Western occultism and our own particular slice of adherence, and inheritance, also. A sorcerer may belong to a tradition but he or she belongs together-with rather than to-that-tradition, as lovers belong with one another, rather than to each other. A true sorcerer may have many teachers, spirit-helpers, spiritual leaders, or even gods, but no master. For the sorcerous perspective by its nature breaks boxes and distorts the edges around categories and whoever becomes a master is also mastered.

The four-element system and the four humours system are boxes. But the punch line is there is no space to place an idea in words that isn't a box. So my story about four dragons will very shortly become a box also. This isn't bad in itself, everything we think about has to go in a box; it is simply the nature of language. But it's a box with less things already in it, it's an old concept at base which is somehow also a less overused box, and so even if we don't choose to believe in it or use it long-term taking a moment to look from the perspective of the box marked 'coloured dragons' affords us a new glimpse of the other systems we're part of. So let us have a closer look at what the box holds.

The Black Dragon

To understand these black serpentine powers we need to delve into the world of the dead and the Underworld in general. The hearth is the centre of the magician's house and it is built over the bones of the dead. In most cases this is no longer literally true, but it remains mytho-logically true. The foundations of your home reach down into the loamy soil of those who have died within and gone down below the flagstones. The profundity of your practice is in the grave, and your manifest mysteries in this world merely as the flower that grows out of it. Memories and flesh have had to rot down for you to get your hands on the stories you are living.

While you savour and enjoy the hard-won fruits of this beautiful-terrible path we walk always remember that everything you are now being nourished by has been upheld by the lives and sacrificial deaths of thousands. This is true even for people who don't practise a magical art but you have the chance to more fully understand it. Before you can feel how the dead are feeding you in this very moment you will not be able to truly get everything you possibly could from the Art. Until you feel the dead in your guts so strongly that to drench the ghosts you need only drink water with consciousness of their many mouths, until you eat the first mouthful of every meal for them, with them, you will not truly have performed necromancy or known the full extent of what initiation can mean.

It will also help us to understand that death is the great initiator of mankind and has washed the eyes of those who are in the Underworld. They have passed into a briny, bloody realm of a shared limbic system. When they have been reweaved in the gut of the Grandmother they are no longer the person you knew in life but something potentially more powerful and knowing. They get this knowledge and potentially even wisdom from their access to states of collectivity. For this reason it is not uncommon to see foremothers who have lived and died in Christian times appear with savage atavisms, especially if they have been dead for some time. The knowledge of the early Mothers works through them, washing in and out tidally. One moment they know you as their grandson, the next they are speaking with the tongues of the ancients, or become the she-wolf.

The other reason for the feeling of primal origins one encounters in Underworld work is that in the memory waters of Annwn all times are *now*, everything is always happening. And if you look at the history of the human race the little part marked 'agriculture' is not really that much more significant in size to the part marked 'industrial age'. We have still spent at least 100 000 years of human existence living as animistic hunter-gatherers, and only the last few thousand being agricultural. Even that has only been in some areas and isn't a particularly generous estimate of what constitutes 'human', one that doesn't take into consideration some other very advanced forms of hominid.

Another explanation might simply be that being earlier, more branches on the human tree of life are descended from those earlier foremothers and there are very many twigs growing upon them. When we come to the crossroads the years burn ... We are all our dead walking. So what does it mean that as a whole, Western culture is collectively so afraid of decay?

We used to carry the dead all night. Yes you read that right, as a proud descendant of Cymric forebears I can say 'we' used to do this, for I am them, and up until not that long ago too. Marie Trevelyan tells us how it was the custom for the coffin to be carried all night, passed from one set of men to the next, the rest all getting drunk as they went. The spirit of Margen (death personified) might have dogged their steps through a dark stony territory in their minds as they marched. For the place between the living and the dead lands takes some walking. It could take between three to nine nights depending on how many pairs of shoes and drinks of water one has offered to others in need throughout their lives. Some people used to take this quite literally and make sure they gave a pair of shoes in perfect condition away to a homeless person to make sure they'd have at least some to wear when they had to make this dread crossing themselves.

As a poetry of living and dying, it isn't perhaps as comforting an idea for some as a sterile light that envelopes you into immediate white-numb in which stands your benevolent, smiling relatives. But the stories a people have told through them by the Unseen tend to be flecked through with the objects of everyday life which that culture surrounds themselves with, as the human mind can only filter things through its own terms and analogies. Our forebears saw a lot of cauldrons and worn out shoes, they knew what it was to thirst and hunger and had in all likelihood at least once offered something to someone in a state of great physical privation.

Cushioned, as most of us in the West are from the direct sight and experience of such things, we should not be surprised that clinically bright lights and anesthetic sentiments reign supreme in the death visions of our age ... But I do not believe this age knows how to tell strong stories that can carry us all night upon their shoulders at our moment of most need ... The stories of this world we've let happen are all about covering over the bruises and post-mortem lividities of life with cosmetics and hiding the evidence of the conqueror worm. Everything about the blackness of the Underworld is shunted away from sight. We fight bitterly against ageing as if it's an obscenity; we are too embarrassed to admit we're still mammals to be comfortable with the wild and painful ecstasies of childbirth or of seeing breastfeeding. We want our dead to have all their fluids sucked out and their holes plugged up so they can't rejoin the Underworld in a gush. We do everything we can to resist the levelling of Death and call this state dignity.

History has hated the Underworld for some time. But whereas some forms of sex are no longer classed as total obscenities by this outrageously dysfunctional era we belong to, death has become the new replacement. Many would now be disturbed by an evening spent carrying a loved one's body in a box, or by the long journey along the corpse path where the coffin must be rested upon each stile, as these were each a mini crossroads.

It would certainly make a difference in how we choose to inter our dead if we held to the story of the First Dead. For in the past in many parts of Britain it was held that whoever was first buried in the graveyard would be doomed to become the graveyard parent and not move on but stay to watch over the doorway between. For this reason good Christian folk would sometimes bury a dog, cat or horse's remains in the site first to prevent any of their people becoming so waylaid. 'Good Christian folk' or not, you have to believe in the Underworld to hold such ideas of long dark journeys made on foot, of thirsty dead that walk certain footways, or guardians of new death sites. Unless we understand that this first death into the land of that site opens a communion between the spirits clothed in red and the denizens of the dead below, allowing a new doorway, the idea of First Dead would make no sense at all. As Dylan Thomas said: 'after the first death, there is no other'.

So whilst our recent ancestors were as mixed up about their feelings towards the very roots of their own life source as we, they tended to focus on the repression of sex and gender expression, and we upon death. For this reason it is wise to take on the previous era's (the Victorian Age) understandings of our weak muscle, whilst ignoring what they have to say about their own area of mass psychosis. It is worth noting, for instance that graveyard dirt didn't have a strictly negative connotation in all British folklore. There is record of people having their limbs buried or even buried up to the neck in the earth of a freshly made grave, with the understanding that the death powers had the ability to take with them the unwanted, as well as the wanted. But today it is common for us to revile and hide from all signals of death's reaping, favouring youth over any signs of maturity and regulating the old death customs out of existence. In such a culture old people become a spectre of the great leveller that is better shunted away from sight.

But before we rush to blame the young for the world the older generations has passed them, one which requires two incomes to participate in society and frequent economic displacement, we should spare a thought for what older folk once brought to the community as a whole as well. The local stories and the folklore are almost no more, as most of us have been displaced and our grandparents themselves were probably displaced from their grandparents and were never passed those stories. What do the old now possess to pass down to us? The chain of mutuality has been broken and they are by and large as lost and unmoored as the young.

Before you start thinking I'm launching into a purely social point here consider our displacement as a society from the location of our people's bones. Who can say that they have around them an immediate environment that contains the bones of their ancestors going back for over a thousand years? If you can say 'yes' to this you are one of the profoundly lucky ones. If you ever think to take for granted the riches upon which you and your family have its roots planted consider your rarity in this world. I have both family history and DNA results to prove that one part of my mother's people have been in the land of Dorset and the surrounding West Country, venturing in and out of Wales, since the end of the last Ice Age. I am the first of her line in all that time to be born here in Australia, upon the most alien possible shore ... This is *hiraeth*, a Welsh word that you would do well to familiarize yourself with if you aren't already. Because it's a neat word from an other than English language that describes not just homesickness but the soul sickness that comes of being displaced from your centre of meaning.

As I have said above the dead create the gravity in our song of ourselves, they pin our story into place in the earth, and become our pole star, our 'true north'. Those of us displaced from our homelands carry this *hiraeth* deep in buried layers inside us; often the ache is far too old for us to even know it's there. Even the recognition of this wound of separation is a healing ache. Allowing ourselves to feel angry along with our ancestors whose graves we can no longer tend, at the same time angry along with and for the displaced shades of the indigenous dead whose land you most likely stand upon if you are in the New World.

It is a wound that can be partially treated but it will take the entirety of this book's content to fully explain how. For now suffice to say you must introduce relics (grave dirt and personal effects) to the earth where you are, but retain enough to make a vessel for one ancestor who is physically present in the soil of your land, through whom all the others may work. Honour all your dead through the local dead. Even if you don't have any bones in the soil as yet you can dowse for the body of someone from the same area as your forebears and work with them. After pouring some offerings upon their grave, given a piece of silver and taken some of the dirt you may make the proposal of adoption to them, so that you can work through the land of that place. Remember, a new opening to the Underworld opens up whenever the dead are buried in large numbers together, so it's important that you have a friend on the local gate.

Understanding the spirits that gather at the crossroads can help us to learn how to manage death better in our own communities. Knowledge of the process of death, the time it takes for each stage of dying to occur and what rites should be done, along with seeing firsthand what happens when one 'wets the shroud' with incessant crying and perpetual grieving, one learns a lot about how it's better for the loved one to love with open hands than clenched fists. For when we let them go into the ground we allow them to become something more than themselves and the love itself is not vulnerable to loss.

It is only when we have internalized all of these differences and manifested as many of them in daily life as can be done (without attracting the attention of the law), that we can really start to embrace the beneficent aspects of the Underworld. There are two arenas where we can best appreciate our animistic ancestors' approach to the giving forces of the Underworld, and that is in the matters of birthing and eating. In the cauldron mythology to be found in Celtic speaking countries we can see a connection between these two types of abundance, that of food and that of babies. One which would never be surprising to anyone who's had subsistence experiences. You have to feed the people before breasts will flow and babies will live to grow up.

The symbols of cauldrons and wells are two of the most common ones to be associated with the beneficial powers of the Underworld, the wells of the unborn, the cauldrons of rebirth and plenty, all echo the ancient understanding of the place below our feet as one of riches that quite literally holds the fat of the land. Although, as the Welsh story of the flooding well near Bala illustrates, what is benevolent in moderation becomes destructive in excess if somebody doesn't know how to put a lid on it. In such stories we find wisdoms for how to understand our own relationship with the ground beneath us, and the mysteries of life springing up from it inside of us.

Because intense Virtue was present both at the moment of birth and of death it was considered important to mark both with the consumption of food. Something about the practice of eating is seen as having a settling and nourishing effect of some kind with Underworldly energies, allowing us to distribute the excess to avoid overflow, to each of the people present. Think of how the groaning cake of the West Country must be shared between all participants at the birth or how a piece of bread and salt was given to the Sin Eater to carry alone, yet a funeral repast is essentially shared between all people present. The eating of food in some way, symbolizing the conversion of death into life, and life into death are very important to most witchcraft mysteries.

It is important that we learn again that in some parts folk believed the corpse candle (orbs of phantom light leaving the body) were red for men or bluish tinged for women, whereas in other areas they believed instead it was a matter of temperament. We need to learn to look for such things and find ways to be with our own dying in a manner appropriate to carrying out the old ways of dying. This is vital both for human health and happiness, which rests on mending our relationship with the black realm.

When someone got chills it was used to be remarked that it was the wind blowing over the feet of the graves, so close did the grave feel to most, now Margen has become an impolite dinner guest that must not be spoken of. It is our challenge to learn how to live again with death. To wear and use again the relics of our dead in ritual, to redden their bones, to feed their skulls, to pour whiskey or rum on their graves and make our understanding of the Underworld festive and joyous.

There is no depth to any joy without a darkness, there is no growth in any Witch House without the understanding that the dead, especially the Mighty Dead, are an immediate part of your community. If you have trouble seeing seemingly 'invisible' people as part of yourself, remind yourself every day that your body is part of all flesh, that all living and dead are part of one heaving organism with you. Carnal knowledge of this organism is called in witchcraft: 'The Sabbat'.

The black dragon could be said to be at war within when there is a great deal of unprocessed, negative ancestral matter hanging around in someone, or even intrusions from the dead. Because we no longer undertake funerals with awareness of Underworldly realities there are many people who think it's good to encourage their dead relatives to stay around, to 'wet the shroud', and otherwise stymie the spiritual progress of their dead. So it's unsurprising, given that hardly anyone feeds or heeds them anymore, that problems within the body of the black dragon are all too common.

The Red Dragon

Initially we will think we know this realm best because we're explicitly, physically part of it. As spirits clothed in red we walk about everyday immersed in the mammalian experience. We live our whole lives requiring a warm steady body temperature and needing to feed our human brains with both calories and stimuli. In these ways we are just like every other animal that bleeds red upon the surface of, or below, the earth. We are, in fact, part of one flesh with them, a giant red serpent of blood and meat.

But we have not been allowed to know this part of ourselves as well as we might initially think. Culture is such a big part of being human that our animal instincts are policed in various ways from day one. So amendable are we as a species to cultural conditioning that it makes sense to see us as the mercurial animal, the culture-creating but also *culture-created* animal ... But no matter how elaborate or restrictive we are with our customs, our inner beast still finds a way to express itself. In this way a successful culture, whether in entire nations or small clans, can be measured against how constructive or destructive the expressions of bestial energy are in that group.

For instance, there are cultures that have been greatly sexually repressed and yet enjoyed gory blood sports. We in the West today are great enjoyers of pornography and have freer access to sexual gratification of one form or another than most other eras, however, many of us would need a lifetime of counselling after a short exposure to medieval style violence. A culture simply decides what it will deem acceptable outlets and what its taboos or obscenities will be. There is no culture that does not have its taboos, but we can perhaps think more about how often we taboo benign activities and actively endorse destructive ones. There are many parents who are far happier for their children to see strong violence than sexuality in a movie, for instance. Most people don't seem to question this cultural norm, it's just meant to be common sense that two people engaged in a loving, pleasurable act would scar a child more than seeing someone's head blown off.

Sadly, Western culture has a cultural inheritance that taboos many perfectly harmless things and quietly (or less so) idolizes many harmful things. This is one of the reasons that you will be asked to slough off a lot in this book, to allow your body's natural intelligence to breathe a little. The part of you that Mary Oliver would call 'the warm soft animal of your body' needs you to take the weight of ideologies off and put down all your anxieties for a moment. To give it time to breathe and try to remember what it loved to feel the caress of before it was told thou shalt not, before it was told to go numb to its quietly, quivering desires that speak an intricate flesh language all through our hair follicles. We need to speak again this ancient language that has all our hair wearing, milk-producing ancestors in it.

In this body language of flesh-soul you see how the red is rooted in the black. For without doing the work that situates you in right relation with your dead and the dead of the land you occupy, what will fertilize the soil where you wish to grow the flower of the spirit? The dead are the compost, the underworld the roots, the plant is the soul, the fertilizing bee is the faerie spouse, the flower is the daimonic awareness, and the fruit is the True Body or Master's Body, at one with itself in Wholeness. As it has collapsed all divisions it is therefore always alive and dead ... eaten and seed spreading ... In different traditions this mastery body has been described as the mystery of Christ or of Buddhahood, Jung called the process Individuation, but the reality behind it cannot be owned by any single tradition, as it is part of the inherent Wholeness potential of mankind.

Culture, just like the beast self, is a double-edged blade, a gift-curse we want to see beyond. We need to leave the one we were brought up in to step outside it before we can really meet our own wild self. The animals are our guides and teachers here.

What may seem to the eyes of the materialist a mere animal wandering by chance, to the eyes of the animistic sorcerer we are seeing the motions of a being more directly connected to the source of life than we are usually aware of being. Our cultures, languages and thought structures partially cut us off, most of the time, from moving with the natural grace and immersion in the One as animals do. They are avatars of potent natural forces. We too are avatars of potent natural forces. But holding the firebrand of the white dragon fire in the way we do means we need to be inducted back into animal understanding by the spirits of the beasts who are our elders in the red realm.

Luckily, the realm of the red dragon is very permeable, and our fetch line or bloodline is usually interpenetrated with the soul force of various animals. These fetch beasts need to be understood as simultaneously an envoy from that animal species that confers upon you certain virtues, but also a mask for ancestrally derived energies. In other words the bear that lives inside you is your grandpa and was his forefather inside him beforehand, but it's also the spirit of bear, which is also the spirit of the land the ancestors lived on.

In my West Country family the idea that a dead loved one could assume an animal form was a taken for granted truth, taken literally all the way down to my grandmother's generation and beyond it to me. The reappearance of my dead grandmother in bird form is one of those everyday miracles that people in rural areas have still hung on to. It is uncertain how seriously the belief is taken, and indeed such ideas cling on in this manner, almost seen as a game by those who engage in them but still done because to do otherwise would be to break covenant with a different kind of truth.

Fiona Macleod's tales of sin eaters speak of the mice leaving the walls if the dead were unsettled. This meant that the dead soul would try to hide his corpse candle in the walls and the mice would leave in fright. Horses were believed to stop before apparitions and it's common knowledge that cats see more than we. But what is fading is the *understanding* of omens. Animals are spirits clothed in red. They have a direct ability to manifest the Otherness in a way our human minds forbid us. When our early forebears painted animals in their caves our anthropologists rushed to assume they were practising hunting magic, projecting our own utilitarian and materialistic values onto them, backwards through time. What if they had tried to think like an animist? Would they not see then that the beasts were gods? Not just because they were predators or prey, or higher or lower on the food chain, but because they were direct eruptions of sacred force before which we stand in need of teaching. The animal spirits each have a unique way of experiencing reality that can unlock certain primal forces in our own animal being, the mercury creature, the great skin-turner that we are as a species.

What do we know when witches were talking to spirits in the form of animals? We know that their understanding of reality was animistic, whatever their professed religion was. The very idea of a powerful spirit in the form of an animal doesn't make sense unless you are. This realm, with its close connection to the black below, has been deeply damaged by the same Puritan society that gave us the witch persecutions and by centuries of terrible human-to-human violence. Mending our relationship to this red dragon power is crucial to forming strong communities, because this is the place where feelings of positive tribalism and oneness arise. Being tutored by the same animal spirit, as with totemic beasts of entire tribes or mystery traditions, was one way of assuring this feeling of oneness at the red level.

Another method is physical grooming and sexuality. Some

people say our species has an inner chimpanzee and an inner bonobo. One side is violent and suspicious of strangers, oppressive of the females, the other peaceful, highly sexual where a lot more power is held especially by elder females. But I would prefer to term this an interaction of the black and red forces within us. The black, usually there to protect us in times of necessary fight or flight which requires the strongest to step forward, misfiring against its own community is the source of the inner chimp. The red serpent is the source of the inner bonobo, who recognises the need for everyone in the group to feel good for they themselves to be at peace and rest easy rather than as the focus of envy, discontent and resentment.

Unlike the chimp metaphor this does not imply that one is desirable and one undesirable, just that they both have their time and their place and can be undesirable outside that context. Sexuality is a wonderful case in point. This force in its healthy state belongs almost entirely to the red serpent that filters or sublimates the black serpent's energies into a form that supports social bonding. However, certain religious and social rulers have decided that this particular type of mammalian bonding activity is, for some seemingly arbitrary reasons shameful and dirty. They have made a sustained attack on the red beast ridden by the Scarlet Woman, one so strong it is hard for us even to imagine a world without it. A world where even the supposedly liberated talk about engaging in 'dirty' or 'naughty' acts when they discuss sex.

Violence, however, is treated as far more suitable for the viewing of young people and as an outlet of tension it has been more popular over the past millennium of human psychosis. The reason the character assassination against sexuality has been so efficient is because of the torture and misshaping of the black serpent, that if abused for long enough tends to shatter or morph into demonic energies, creating a snowball-of-destruction effect. We will return to this destruction snowball effect and how to halt it later when we talk about our urgent need to placate the Underworld.

When the red serpent feeling of togetherness and oneness that come from physical contact is shamed it tends to retract in pain, leaving the black serpent to defend it. When sexuality is driven purely by the black realm it tends to become selfish and maybe even aggressive in nature. At its best it objectifies or adopts a passive strategy to get control, because the black serpent's existence is all about getting control. Not because it's an evil or pernicious force as most religions characterize all dark things, but because it's only meant to be deployed in service of one's own life instinct. It's there to defend our boundaries against attack and unleash our fight or flight behaviour.

In its right relation, it's a beautiful natural disaster at work showing the individual's deep inner power and drive to live. But when it's unleashed in the wrong places, such as in an activity that is meant to be a form of social bond making or grooming (sex), it has a negative effect. Humans who have been shamed for their natural impulses since birth tend to have their red serpent retract, after that sexual drives can appear quite unpleasant in nature and thus it goes in a circle, with this outcome proving the 'nasty' nature of sexuality. Just as we were told in the first place! See? Didn't that feel dirty and selfish? See look, this is why we should be more puritanical because sex is clearly dangerous to communities and tears them apart! Well of course it does when all you ever get to see are eruptions of hunger coming from repressed, touch-starved people bleeding from shame wounds! It clearly rips holes in the social fabric because it promotes jealousy and predation ... Well of course the starving are jealous of the morsel and do not act well when moving from a place of desperation ... But what if we weren't starving?

This is like giving someone a disease and then using the unpleasant symptoms of the disease to prove why it was right to infect them in the first place! Or discriminating against a class or race of people for so long they fall into poverty then using their own degradation as proof they were always inferior ... Until we can come to terms with the fact our natural animal self, when it isn't shamed or degraded, wants for perfectly innocent pleasures that are, when fully participatory between all parties, as blameless as eating or drinking, how are we ever going to stop placing ourselves above other animals? If we think it's perfectly acceptable for animals to have sex in the field outside but shocking and disgusting if it were humans, at some level we still think we are superior to them. We still see ourselves as the exception, the exceptional ones with a culture that is basically asserted by our ability to dominate our animal selves and then the animal selves of others, human and non-human alike.

Now of course there are practical social and legal ramifications to actually having sex in public, but in theory we should certainly consider why this is? Cultures of any kind that seek to fully dominate rather than learn from the animal self are noticeable for their tight regulations on sexuality. In humans the togetherness instinct triggered by the red serpent moving through and forming 'group fetch' is a precondition for shared magical experiences. Of course you don't have to have sex with everyone in your community to create this kind of connectivity. But the very fact we are so suspicious of sexuality and the abuse of it in magical and religious orders shows that we immediately associate sexuality with the black serpent, and that we think of sex when the word we're looking for is *abuse.* Sex is not suspicious or corrupt, *abuse* is suspicious and corrupt, the very fact this distinction is so difficult for us to understand is symptomatic of the larger problem. It is symptomatic of the fact we have likely had far more to do with abuse than normal sexuality, especially in spiritual or religious communities.

There is nothing truly 'sexual' about sexuality that leads from the black serpent; it is merely a form of disguised abuse and predation, a cloak for domination of another's will. Just as many have rightly remarked that rape is more about aggression than it is sexuality. Abuse in covens or magical orders should not be deemed enough respect as to be called a 'sexual' matter, it does not deserve to be linked with a practice involving the giving and receiving of pleasure. It should be called what it is, an act of taking from, oppressing, stealing from and dominating another human being, and in many cases it should just be called assault.

True sexuality, as expressed through the togetherness impulse of the red serpent, is inclusive and wishes to merge with other things to remember the state of One Flesh. This is the opposite to the desire to place something lower than yourself, because how do you do that when you have become one thing with them? Regardless of who is physically on top and on bottom or how vigorous the act, how can you see as less than yourself something you are one with? The red serpent of lust swallows, devours and assimilates you in a sexual act with someone else or others. If this is not so then the act is something done *to* one of the people by the other person and likely possesses the seeds of Ownership and its twin, Violence.

This violence, of course will likely be invisible at first to all who have been raised in a culture of implied violence. This violence may not be physical but can be any act where power was stolen from you without your full and knowing consent. If you are asking yourself if a relationship between yourself and a teacher, mentor, leader or student is potentially abusive then the answer is probably 'yes'. If the innocence of true bonding had been present in the room neither party would be inclined to even ask the question. Even the bent and damaged human heart knows deep down, if it's honest with itself, when it's been in the presence of true capital-L Love and when it's being stolen from. Nonetheless it can take a while spent outside of abusive contexts for this instinctual, inner intelligence to start speaking to us again.

Healthy sexual relationships allow the people to productively sublimate the energies of their black serpent drives into red serpent playfulness. Please understand when I say 'play' that I recognise that healthy adult humans, particularly witches, play hard at times! Take BDSM for example, a practice where the black serpent drives to dominate or submit and its responses to pain and adrenalin are played with by the red serpent with the loving motivation of sharing pleasure with one's partner and exercising rather than exorcising the black dragon.

If one understands the vast difference in the two drives and which is in charge, it's impossible not to see the wide gulf between the healthy and the abusive manifestation. The fact that many are confused by the differences shows how little we understand what true consent is and what a big deal it is. It shows how much we still want to police the behaviour of others with our ancestral inner puritan. (Spoiler alert: we all have one in there.)

For those who feel unclear, here is the difference in root motivation between abuse and a consensual loving act that might look savage. One desires to genuinely degrade and control another human being to prop up their own fears of not being in control of a frightening universe, the other has learned to play with these impulses and disempower the more pernicious ones, similarly to how sparring and play wrestling with a friend are not the same thing as going out to truly injure or disable an opponent. If you can understand the difference between the BDSM versus abuse example, or the sparring versus combat one, then you can understand the difference between healthy sexual relationships within your community and unhealthy ones.

The Glas Dragon

When it comes to responding to the green realm in a non-judgemental and non-hierarchical manner we don't have the option of simply refusing to eat beings of this realm. The human body doesn't do well without input from the green. So at some point we will have to come to terms with the notion of loving consumption and gratitude formulating a ritual consciousness that sublimates our predatory desires via the transformative medium of sanctity, even if we prefer to keep this loving savagery for those with no faces.

You won't get along with this realm by trying to say you aren't taking life when you eat it or that their lives are lesser than the lives of things you share a blood colour with. Until you genuinely approach this ancient kingdom of life as though it is just as valuable to you as things with eyes and faces that look like yours, your experience of faerie life will be greatly hampered. The Fair Folk are, if nothing else, fair, and they tend to return tit for tat. If you act as if their lives are of lesser value than yours by carelessly destroying one of their trees they will act as though you yourself are a lesser life form, and careless destroy you with an elf dart that will show up as a medical malady. When faeries decide they are not on good terms with you few things will blossom or flourish around you for long.

Like most of these realms there are large problems that lie between us and adopting a helpful mindset for dealing with them. Cornelius Agrippa noted that the credulous and innocent sort of folk is best at seeing and communing with faeries. Implying that it takes a certain naïve openness to life, and instinctual belief-belief. Fundamentally everything that faerie-touched individuals tend to be are the very things that our current society excoriates. Imagination, play, creativity, spontaneity, these thing have all been trivialized and seen as lacking in utilitarian value and when that's not happening they are being preyed upon by those ridden by black serpentine drives.

This is because we judge all other orders of life based on rules that are not so much species centric, but centric to the culture we've developed, which in this case is global capitalism. The things that faerie influence has to bring are just not as valuable as wood chip and mentally-colonised workers who don't waste time on flights of fancy. I have spoken more about the pernicious aspects of this green realm shaming in my book *Sounds of Infinity: Witchcraft and the Faerie Faith.*

In short, the problem with this style of thinking is that much like with sexuality in the red realm it attacks some of the most delicious and potent aspects of life, things that happen to also be deeply nutritious and empowering to the human soul. The green realm could be compared to both the Fruit on the Tree of Knowledge and the paradise serpent, that libidinal drive towards Knowing, the force that tempts us away from the world of humans into the dream of the planet; the force that nourishes our inner world ... But, like the herbs in Ceridwen's cauldron when brewed and refined only the first three drops contain wisdom, the rest poison. Mankind's greatest achievements arise when they manage to dance successfully with the great green Leviathan who preceded us here upon the earth, the red and the green mutually devouring each other in a circle of sustenance and rebirth. We must learn again the steps to that dance before it's too late.

In return for learning the strange backwards seeming ways of the faerie kingdom, this realm holds the keys to our very sanity. There is no way to reconcile the Underworld of us with the Upperworld within, that currently acts as overlord over most of our mental processes, without this misty synthesizing power. Otherwise we become a polarized nightmare of a species, stuck in a bipolar tug-of-war between a materialistic rational brain and uncontrolled fear and aggression outbursts.

A key example of their necessity can be found in many spiritual traditions. The moment you perceive that the ideals of a tradition (inflicted from above as ideas and belonging to the whiteness of being) as being out of kilter with the true feelings, instincts, fears and insecurities of the people (black realm) you can see what we have done in forgetting the Third Way, in reducing our world to a binary between up/down, good/evil, heaven/hell. Even those traditions that might seemingly reject or critique such binaries still often exhibit this tension between the real and the ideal in their communities, even manifesting as outright hypocrisy among many members. This like all the social ills I've chosen to draw attention to here is a leading cause of weakened communities.

Most people are used to adherence. They've grown up somewhere they were expected to adhere to and parrot back certain principles regardless of whether or not they could actually act on them, and so they continue this pattern. Catholicism has created a whole religious structure focusing on ritual humiliation around the inability of its members to live up to the standards inflicted from above upon the primal self: confession, followed by absolution and then more falling short. This story has permeated our culture so deeply that it is often thought that most well-known occultists' magical lives don't actually live up to the hype. It can be a source of surprise for some when they discover someone actually practising what they preach.

The green realm, those who open for us this liminal area that leads to neither Heaven nor Hell, can teach us how to mediate the space between ideals and manifesting them in reality. If the way you are actually living falls short of how you ideally visualise your magical life then the green serpent and you could have a fruitful conversation. Without the Fair Folk's good graces, this grace inside ourselves is likely to remain dormant like our own interior plant life.

Even though the green realm is not as obviously present in the human body as the other three we breathe the product of it, we are nourished by the vegetation of it, we have for millennium consumed medicines and plant teachers from there. When we began to destroy the forests, we attacked the wilderness within ourselves. When we made laws to try to prevent the plant teachers from interacting with mankind we launched a cultural genocide against imagination and against inspiration. This realm could yet save us all, if we but remembered how to listen ... Faeries are depicted as small for a reason. In truth they can be any size they want to be. But it is the small almost unnoticed, hidden folk and their seeming whimsy that holds the keys to unlocking the dilemma of the gulf between the ideal and the real. They are little because to see them you have to *pay attention.*

Consider yourself, and your magical practice as a tree. Your branches aspire towards the light. Their greatest wish is to come to flower or fruit, to be caressed by the delicate feet of bees, to be part of making honey, to be part of throwing down seeds for the future. Meanwhile your roots are deep in the earth, feeding on death. Without the black realm you won't have the nourishment or the stability to reach up and drink in the stars. But to someone who didn't understand a tree at all it would seem like these parts have an opposite agenda. The roots and the branches appear to grow in a different direction, the roots seek greater depth and search out underground water sources; the branches seek greater height and crave the touch of the light. This is such simple ecology in action that it's remarkable how many spiritual traditions still get by in demonizing one direction and upholding the other!

Like the trunk that holds it all together, the faeries of the woods and the other green realm courts are involved in processing and synthesizing, making two seemingly contrary agendas work as a glorious whole. No wonder theirs is the third road, for they are indeed creatures of synthesis. For the tree, the Wholeness we call Mastery of our Art is easily obtained for she is eternally in a state of meditation and needn't worry about the distractions of large or fast physical movements.

But for us as a person or a community, we need to work on this creative realm where life is continually turned into art, and art is transmuted into greater life, because it is there, in the realm of story and myth where the real and the ideal can meet up and become healthily synthesized. We were not meant to be reduced to a raw nerve of instinct covered over by a white realm ideal that eternally whips the black serpent of us into form with its demands for perfection, and when that is unobtainable, shame. The green serpent knows how to take us from a state of paradisiacal innocence to one of self-knowledge through the beauty and seduction of art, music and storytelling. He is the subtle Master of 'skillful means'.

Our occult community should always honour these holy rituals of creativity. It is one thing to host the occasional bardic circle but we still live in a world that talks about UPG (unverified personal gnosis) as though the realm of magic were a science that can or should be verified, but if we truly respected the numinous world of the imagination, we would begin showing our respect to the faerie world by taking up use of words like 'imaginal', imagination that is understood to be real. Because this is the realm that Faerie Sight exists in. There is no such thing as a gnosis which is false, on powerful and less powerful stories. Stories show they are powerful stories by people taking them on board, this is the only verification they need. Faeries talk to you via the imaginal realm; if you've spent serious time in nature without too much mental chatter you've probably heard them. You probably mistook their communications for some random fertile imaginings and sudden inspirations that you thought of as your own. When you spoke about them to the wider community you were probably told they were your UPG, but whatever scientific sounding name someone comes up with it's important to remember that every story starts off unverified, and every religion or mystical path starts off with a story.

While we are still imagination-shaming those who dare to follow visions that haven't been suitably 'verified', or making hard-nosed, abrasive calls for such things, we may fail to hear the quiet voices of those who have been truly faerie-touched, they don't always tend to be the people who are shouting back at you in favour of their UPG. But this behaviour does more than just silence the sensitive. There is always the risk of beginning to hear the voice of the critic asking for proof half way through one's own experiences.

This of course doesn't mean that we must relinquish a love for quality. There are always strong stories and less strong stories. Strong stories are like strong trees, they have just enough blackness and rot in them to give them substance and the grit of the earth, they have a strong trunk which is proven by the fruit of the flower. The seeds that it sends out that can grow in other people's soil show the value of the story. From the faerie perspective, instead of UPGs and VPGs ('verified' personal gnosis) there are only stories, which humans use to synthesize their primal urges with their ideals, and there are myths. A myth is a story that has legs. It works for more than one person. And when I say it works, I mean it is a story that transforms lives. To a faerie, who deals with the power of synthesis and passing the membrane between inner and outer, it is this power, not the supposedly objective nature of scientific truth, which makes a vision arising from the imaginal, worthwhile. You might say they have their eyes on a different prize ...

As you can imagine there are a lot of habits of mind that are praised in our society that are toxic to the faerie people that are like the energetic equivalent of cold iron. From Agrippa's quote below about what kind of people can interact easily with faeries, you can see that everything our society respects is less attractive to Them than the things we tend to make fun of:

> ... that which is especially to be observed in this, the singleness of the wit, innocency of the mind, a firm credulity, and constant silence; wherefore they do often meet children, women, and poor and mean men. They are afraid of and fly from men of a constant, bold, and undaunted mind ...

They don't care for and aren't impressed by the things that make a human powerful in our realm; in fact the tables are entirely turned. It's our capacity for surrender, grace, receptiveness, imagination, strong-vulnerability, wonder and awe that make us powerful or attractive from a faerie's perspective.

One can imagine that the bold and forthright have something in them much like the feel of iron. Faeries do not appear to those who go forcefully seeking to meet them. Their behaviour can best be understood via the story of Rhiannon whose horse always got further away the more Pwyll used his iron to spur his horse on faster and with greater determination. When he but surrendered and humbly asked her to wait, there she stayed. You will find that the seeming simplicity of Faerie may be one of the hardest mindsets for modern folk to experience.

To begin healing the relationship with this realm we need not only to stop cutting down trees as if it were somehow not a killing, and to stop privileging the life of things with faces over these more mysterious beings whose faces we don't understand how to see yet, we need to change our habits of thinking, to almost reverse them. Only then when we are able to do this will we begin to learn how to open up conduits and roads between the Underworld depths of our impulses and the Whiteness. In this healing work potentially lies the death of unproductive shame and a remedy for the demonizing of the black realm.

The White Dragon

You may imagine I'm going to say we're all right with the spirits of this realm. You would think so after nearly two millennium of monotheism and its sky realm worship, full of angels ... But if anything, we have misunderstood this realm most terribly of all and our whole culture is a misshapen testament to our distortion of it. We have deformed it out of shape by removing it from its context. I am going to talk a lot about context-dependent realities throughout this book, as it's an important part of the concept of spiritual ecology that underpins animistic thinking.

If you consider the human body as a glyph, the Upperworld

and the Heavens are clearly located in the head. This is context, because a head must exist in relation to a body. There is no way to imagine one without one as consciousness as we know it is experienced in the sensory field, in other words our perception as we know it is shaped by the fact we have a body not just a head. So in this way it isn't surprising that whilst the West has transitioned away from being governed by theocracy, or state sanctioned religion, we have not fully removed this focus. We still privilege the head over all other parts of the body. The Enlightenment only changed our answer to why the brain was most important. Beforehand, the human brain was the crowning glory of creation because it allowed mankind to become aware of God.

After the Enlightenment we tended to elevate Reason to the position that God had previously held, and still we lauded the light. There has never yet been a celebrated Endarkenment! In fact we use the term 'Dark Ages' to speak of a time when history went out, when less records were kept. Despite the fact that the post-Enlightenment centuries have been the bloodiest in human history, we also have the cheek to associate the Dark Ages with violence and barbarism. I would in fact argue that the real problem with implementing the Enlightenment's promises of the kind of world it would deliver is that mankind's capacity for pure reason or logic is greatly hampered by the damage that has been done to our ability to synthesis darkness. The darkness we have denied as a civilization is already chewing away at the foundation of the modern world, try as we might to locate it only in the figure of the other, the terrorist or the infidel ...

The most obvious example of this exists in current world events. Science, the work of the unfettered intellect, tells us with alarmingly high levels of agreement between experts that **if we don't act soon, we are heading for imminent ecological collapse of a scale not seen before in the lifetime of our species.** But does simply knowing these facts and presenting them to the public cause immediate action? Are people rushing to fix the problem like it's our number one priority because reasonably speaking you don't have much room for other issues if your area can't sustain life anymore? No. In fact we've been stalling for so long we are close to being past the point of no return. Why, if reason alone could ever be mankind's saviour, should this be the case?

Well, reason alone is not god of mankind as much as some may wish it, despite what the monotheistic God who we never truly dethroned but just changed his name to 'Cosmos' or 'Logic', will tell you. We still function as if our minds were St Michael with his spear, violently and with all associated machismo, thrusting light down the throat of ignorance and superstition. This is all that's needed to address the problems of the world. Right? We just need to fully colonise the rest of the barbaric world with Western rationalism, thrust that spear home a little harder, and all the suicide bombers and abortion clinic shooters will suddenly realise their folly …

The problem is, whichever form of cutting away part of the human psyche we choose to engage in, the body-shaming cutting away of the thou-shalt-not model or the imaginal-shaming world of atheism, we remain an animal perfectly suited to the habitat in which it evolved with a brain that hasn't changed a great deal in the past eighty thousand years or so. Part of us is still a wolf, being made to live like a dog whilst expected to become an android.

Most people who subscribe to the ongoing Enlightenment project appear to enjoy the occasional self-deprecating moment of admitting we are hairless apes. It seems to be assumed that through rationalism we can simply sublimate whatever pesky primal urges we are left with. Or at least the proponents seem to think *they* can. A position that is often contrasted in seemingly ego-gratifying ways with the ignorant masses who cannot so easily get a handle on their base, animalist and superstitious leftover mental software! The only problem with atheist materialism is 'those people' who can't, and still can't are very, very many ... The dangerous Other who is less-than has just moved locations, and feeling superior might be fun for a bit, but it sure isn't going to fix the problems we face.

It is never considered that if so many people have such trouble yielding their experiential perceptions to the atheist materialist angle there could be a problem with the model itself. It certainly doesn't seem to have any tools in its arsenal other than scorn and repetition of facts to try to change the situation. Personally I love facts too, but observation shows they don't sway the mind of most humans, and making people feel afraid only causes paralysis. Clearly humans require something more than the statement of facts to radically change their lives.

Any position that believes it has the one and only valid angle on truth and doesn't seem to mind if eighty to ninety per cent of the world will fail to make the cut for internalizing its principles has lost touch with human nature. Whilst atheism, the rising creed of our times, indeed seems to do no bombing or persecution it also possesses no answers the bulk of humans will find satisfying to their whole selves. Whether it's by religion or logic as long as the head is allowed to dominate rather than dance with the rest of the body, that which is above will always be given more respect than that below and with such a mindset we will destroy our own foundations, as we are doing. For to scorn and dominate as the head may do, it doesn't get anywhere without that which carries it around.

What if the problem here has nothing to do with empirical exploration of the cosmos, agnostic curiosity or technology but in the framework inherited from the Enlightenment, which had already bent the Whiteness out of shape? What if this inheritance has made it intensely difficult for us to appreciate the other dimensions of ourselves whilst it distorted our perception of spirits of the white realm? When the sun casts down his fiery spears and is drunk up hungrily by the green realm that then gives us oxygen, do you imagine he does so in violence in the belief he's penetrating an inferior? What if the penetration of the dragon by the spear of St Michael was reimagined as an act of union? The light of the heavens being sacrificed into the hungry mouth of the Underworld ... Could we wield the light of our intellect with humility, patience and awe to observe our other functions as equals rather than as inferiors? In this imaginative self-discipline and tempered humility we would see again the true brilliance of the white realm. Because it never went away, we just grasped so hard at it, light hungry as we were that we bent it out of shape in our hands.

This is what we have forgotten about the sky (that we have made Overlord without consulting him), how much it desires to fall like the angels ... How much it desires to spill its sunlight and its starlight into the inky darkness of forever. How much it desires to quench the soil with its sky waters.

The reason of man has the same capacity. To give joy and nourishment to the other aspects of the self, to shine light on them and receive new nuances of enjoyment thereby, to lend meaning to the life of the senses and intuitions rather than to oppress them; for the consciousness to not control or denigrate the senses but to sit before them as a student before a teacher and ask them to instruct us. Although Sky/Mind/Above/Dominant has been made the king upon the throne, as a principle the Whiteness is more like the flowers and fruit of the tree, made to be plucked, eaten and assimilated by the body to her greater fruitfulness. Like stars the sky/mind is made to reach high and then to fall. Light is sacrificial not authoritarian, and in misunderstanding this we have distorted leadership and teaching of all types.

For consciousness in no way can be separated from the sensorium of the body, but, owes everything to this chance to reflect upon itself via the mirror of the other. This fundamental folly, this belief that somehow we could pluck off aspects of human nature in favour of one, discard the roots, trunk and branches and still arrive at the fruit, is typical of a society that values the outcome of capital more than the human lives that make up the means to production. We want the outcome of something without process; we want consciousness without giving value to the senses that allow us to be conscious of being conscious. From these misunderstandings flow the beginning of the fully ripened problem our species now faces. Unbridled greed for the end product and willingness to denigrate the means (even when the 'means' has a face) in favour of this end, a demon force that arises when the black realm is not satiated, came along next to seal the deal with our self-destruction. This twisted relationship between the realms became so intense that it manifested and began to be acted out on the stage of human history.

Racial whiteness was created out of what had once been a myriad of culturally diverse peoples who just happened to have roughly the same skin tone, and created to contrast the notion of 'blackness', a notion of homogeneity that was also constructed out of various culturally diverse groups. Like a strange crooked mirror to the Otherworld, the people designated with blackness became the literal means of production, exploited to produce for the white man via the age-old evil of slavery. The reductive heart of the evil at work here can be well understood just through seeing our willingness to reduce whole human beings to 'standing for' a colour in the first place ... when each human being by his or her own sovereign nature holds the latent or blossoming potential for all the colours. No human was ever meant to stand for 'white' or 'black', just as no human being was ever meant to be reduced to an expression of 'masculinity' or 'femininity' but instead contain the potential for all Wholeness waiting to lean into itself. Why are we so afraid of extending that Wholeness to others? To treat them as the Wholeness they are still becoming? What does it take from us to remove the weight of our perception from their beingness?

As a society we try to cure things in the realm of action and politics before we've even taken the time to understand what the problem is we're actually facing. All spiritual healers understand that an evil must first be defeated in the realm of spirit before a physical result can be expected. Everything we experience is rooted in the body and we must approach the innate intelligence of this ancestral congregate with humility. But humility was not present in the text that told us to go forth and subdue nature, nor is it present in the belief that we might seek to unlock all the secrets of nature when we have not yet fathomed the mystery of ourselves and have pushed aside the indigenous bearers of wisdom in favour of what we've 'discovered', which is mere knowledge. You can know all the facts about how the universe works but if you haven't wisdom enough to discover Right Relations with things then your smugness in the face of superstition will be remembered by your descendants as a hubris that came right before your culture's fall.

But humility is not possible without perspective and this is the great and much abused gift of the white realm. The ability to widen one's view, placing events and feelings in wider contexts, is a gift from the spirits of the whiteness. It is never about detachment it is more about sharpness and complexity of vision. There is a daimonic gaze that cannot be clouded by sentiment, one that sees the relationship between things. It is powerful in the extreme and our culture has become intoxicated by its ultra-violet to white fire, it has baked most of our brains so that we no longer know its true flavour like someone whose taste buds are weak from over stimulation. For the Whiteness also knows when to rise up and when to lay itself down in offering before the intelligence of the body and congregate of the ancestors. Its ability to rise up and take in the eagle's view is only complete and perfected in witness of its self-offering and desire to make the abyss pregnant with its lightning-fall of sacrifice.

The spirits of this realm have been as much abused by our

way of seeing as the faeries have, for we have generated them into sexless, emotionless, faultless, angels. A mere caricature of our futile desire to be outside our animal natures ... Like with any of the spirits we've discussed here, the best way we can open ourselves wider to hearing the voice of the spirits of the whiteness is through systematically healing the distortions in our view of them. By misshaping the true solar hero we've robbed him of his descent into the Underworld, his love of it, his union with it, his vulnerability, his bleed out, his sacrifice, his bridge-making of his own body, his tithe-paying to the darkness and the parts where the darkness forged and honed him to be strong. By doing that we've not only done damage to those powers in ourselves but our relationship with those powers.

Some of us try to correct this by veering away from the white serpent realm or away from what we call the masculine. By denying them and focusing instead on the Underworld, the black realm, so called 'low' magic and folk customs only, or perhaps working exclusively with goddesses. But an overemphasis which led to a distortion can't be properly fixed by a swing in the opposite direction. This, our reason would be able to tell us, if we hadn't so overtaxed that part by repressing the darkness it needs to the extent that our reason is no longer functioning very well.

Demons arise when the darkness is repressed and exorcised rather than exercised, and the white realm spirits do indeed have the ability to immolate demons, just by opening the burning eyes of all-seeing perspective that they carry in their wings. But before it can do so it must be nourished by its relationship with the whole web of life, it must be wetted a little, held and suckled by the darkness. Its nature is true perfection when it is earthed ... It will need the faerie realm to sweeten and stimulate it too, so it can learn subtlety and skill. In this whole process the seemingly dominant and pushy Whiteness/Consciousness must learn to become receptive and passive, to bend and flow and become the student of Sovereignty, the great force of holiness that is present in Land which our bodies are also one with, and are both spirits' homes of the ancestors.

I am not the first to analyze Cu Chulainn as a failed hero but here I will take it further and suggest we see him as Consciousness itself, in regards to being a spirit of the Whiteness, facing the Morrigan, who represents the senses where the body's awareness crosses a threshold into the unconscious aspect of our being and the earth/ancestors. The Morrigan, the body's black-red knowing, keeps appearing to Cu Chulainn, the consciousness, in different animal and human guises trying to get his attention. Just as the body may seem to betray us with illnesses we can't understand, it seems almost like the Morrigan is out to get Cu Chulainn. But to understand why this power of sovereign body-awareness would try so hard to envelope the hero we need only understand the kind of consciousness that Cu Chulainn represents.

Cu Chulainn is consciousness turned up to the level of titanic self-assertion. He is a single principle that resists all other principles so violently that he is ultimately on a path to self-emollition. The symbolism is all there. When plunged into a vat of icy water to try to cool his 'warp spasms' of warlike fury, his body heat explodes the vat. When women attempt to soften and sweeten him by baring their breasts to him, instinctually understanding that he needs to come back to body, he covers his eyes. His white fire tries to resist grounding itself and yet paradoxically creates swathes of death, which result in 'walls made of corpses'. Just like this out of control white fire does in the modern world and every other culture it has taken hold of.

He fights with numerous female warriors and his forms of 'defeating' them are very telling. One warrior-woman, Aife, he defeats and leaves pregnant, seemingly as a reminder of who is on top. The other, Medb, he is able to defeat because she gets her period on the battlefield. The message seems to be here that the solar hero can assert himself over the feminine no matter how powerful because of the weakening association with these lower Underworld forces connected to reproduction.

The solar hero, associated always with heat and dryness, and hostile to wetness and coolness, not only seems invincible but his behaviour sets out a dare to the natural world, almost literally taunting it to try to bring him back down to the earth. Some part of him reaches out for death if not health, anything to readdress the over-balance he is living. The death-drive seems to be the final way the over-heated solar hero reaches for the earth. Enter, the Morrigan …

Here we realise that a different story about the feminine is telling itself almost subversively through this myth, like a cross weave story with older substrata in the narrative's archeological foundations. The Morrigan has her own agenda. She doesn't come to Cu Chulainn out of some mere sadism, no, she comes to him attracted by his hero light. Sovereign forces are attracted not repelled by the hero light around a man, but this man needs to learn what heroes are for … All can still be well for him if he moves past his eye covering behaviour and responds to the women's intuition that his light must, needs to, be grounded in the body's sensuality. *It still isn't too late for him.* His 'warp spasm' battle fury is described in terms that leave little to the post-Freudian imagination.

> The first warp-spasm seized Cúchulainn, and made him into a monstrous thing, hideous and shapeless, unheard of. His shanks and his joints, every knuckle and angle and organ from head to foot, shook like a tree in the flood or a reed in the stream. His body made a furious twist inside his skin, so that his feet and shins switched to the rear and his heels and calves switched to the front ... On his head the temple-sinews stretched to the nape of his neck, each mighty, immense, measureless knob as big as the head of a month-old child ...

Everything about this image not only records a feeling of immense distortion which becomes monstrous in its intensity but a kind of bursting hot, hyper erect, vein-popping fullness which clearly is much like the Otherworld's version of 'roid-rage'.

Sensing this, the Morrigan comes to him before a conflict claiming to be the daughter of a local king and offers to lay with him. Given the details that he is in a new area and the woman presents as a king's daughter this is not just an offer of sex but an offer from Sovereignty to submit himself in marriage with the land. He says no ... Commentators intent on reducing the Morrigan to a peevish girl whose ego has been damaged, read her as going after him because she's offended by his refusal. It is this license given to the oppressor (within us and without) to decide who will be trivialized and who will be made ridiculous that stands between us and our ability to activate these myths inside us. The Morrigan doesn't represent the female sex and Cu Chulainn the male, this would be a terrible and dangerous misunderstanding of the black realm, one that both the protagonist and the reader will ultimately pay for.

The Morrigan begins, despite his slights not because of them, to instruct Cu Chulainn to not punish him, for such are the Right Relations between his realm and hers. His resistance is a sign of his great need for her. She appears as an eel and causes him to trip in a ford when in battle, showing him how that which is beneath one's feet and interest can sometimes be that which pulls a whole structure down ... But he is unable to hear her pre-verbal language and lashes out in anger and breaks her ribs. Next she tries to show him by appearing as something more fearsome, the wolf. This is when a wise man would have seen the black realm going on the defensive, but he his not a wise man. Still he does not respect her and puts out one of her eyes with a slingshot. Finally she appears as a heifer, a creature that relentlessly gives to mankind, giving him one last chance to honour that which sustains him, and he breaks her leg.

When his battle is over, Consciousness who has now becoming over-weening Ego, meets the intelligence of the Land/Body again, this time the Morrigan is in the form of an old woman milking a cow, for sovereignty is everywhere and can never be avoided. She still bears the injuries that he gave her in the three animal forms. But she gives him three drinks of milk and upon each one he blesses her. Just as Coleridge's ancient mariner blesses the slimy creatures of the deep. As consciousness blesses the body/land the injuries immediately disappear. Cu Chulainn fails to understand the extra chance he's been given or to see how the Underworld is always reaching out to restore balance and will only tip the balance in favour of retribution when denied and denied and denied ... He tells the Morrigan that he'd have not blessed her if he knew it was her ... Yet the Morrigan has demonstrated her fundamental power that he can never overcome, despite all his strength and hero light, *every time you thank anything for anything you automatically bless her.*

It is only when those sovereign forces in the land/body/Underworld have reached out in every form they could that they choose illness and death. Now the Morrigan is forced to offer Cu Chulainn dog meat. It is interesting after what we've hinted at regarding wolves and dogs that Cu Chulainn's fate is so bound up with that of the captive canine. He is caught between his own taboo on the eating of dog meat and a taboo in breaking hospitality. What a host offers you, you must eat and so rather than lose face he eats the dog meat and seals his fate. Even as Cu Chulainn is dying he still resists the earth and has himself tied to a standing stone so that he might die still erect and not willingly surrender his blood-seed to the womb-tomb of the ground.

Cu Chulainn, in being a tale about the over-extended solar hero is very much a metaphor for our own excesses as a culture and what we have idealized. Although Cu Chulainn performs horrid excesses of violence, much of which against female figures, he is upheld as a hero because our society still wishes to promote that which is on top over that which is below. The bias is even in the language, try wording the former sentence without using an 'over' to describe holding something as more important.

Part of us still admires the over-extended solar-hero for his adamant refusal to lie down, his total rejection of the yielding, of the feminine, of the softer bodily influences that are craved by his rage distorted, vein-pumping, unsatisfied flesh. His is the violence that has torn our world apart, and yet still we unconsciously heap our offerings on his shrine of the monstrosity of unfettered Ego assertion.

Yet none of this is what the story was meant to be about, the warrior daimon of the sky worlds has always been lightning falling to earth and fecundating storms he spends himself … Like all the spirits he can't make any healthy sense in our lives outside of his context, and his context involved the Morrigan, who stands in for the Underworld and the even more ancient hag goddesses of the land.

If we can understand what has gone wrong with our view of the sky realms and the Whiteness we can understand what so often goes wrong in our perception of leadership and knowledge. Because of this extreme solar hero figure and his obsession with 'power over', untempered by sacrifice or sensuality, we have come to think that leadership is the same thing as hierarchy. We imagine all leaders (either of groups or thought-leaders such as academics) as an extension of this dominance myth which, I might add, Cu Chulainn is only one example of.

Leadership in the truly sovereign sense arises from the Underworld, from below, it calls for someone to lay themselves down upon her, not raise themselves up above. It calls for us to make a bridge of ourselves. Yet largely we do not know how to encourage this behaviour in our leaders let alone how to bring it forth from ourselves, we sidestep the problem by claiming we don't really need leaders. Just as some of us try to sidestep the problem of our distorted relationship with the Upper World by only focusing on the Underworld ... or claim we don't really need men and have all-female communities. Yet, regardless, everything is within everything else, if you tunnel long enough in the Underworld you'll eventually need to confront the sky. You cannot get away from an overused principle by swapping to its opposite and ignoring it, as it still holds its echoes in the totality of you. You can reject men or reject women, but what will you do with the latent one inside you?

Groups without any kind of leadership stay that way in name only. It only takes a casual look at any kind of group work to see that when no leadership is given by those with more knowledge (i.e. for instance the lecturer at university) groups naturally look towards the most dominant or pushy individual to organise everyone or in rarer cases someone who sounds smart. The truth is not that we can do away with leaders, it just isn't how human groups work, but that we need to reimagine them. We need to see that leaders and masters are not the same thing. We need to see that we don't know how to encourage leadership that isn't based on hierarchy in our communities because *our conditioned mindset tells us to disrespect whatever we can walk over.* And yet King Bran of Welsh myth passed to us the wisdom that he who would lead must make of himself a bridge.

How will there ever be any bridges when we have worshipped the over-powers to such a degree that the maiden whose lap the feet of the ruler sits in to draw his power is no longer recognised as the true source of power? That the holy whore who lets others on top of her is saddled with the ass's collar and made fun of, that the man who allows himself to be penetrated is seen as less of a man because he lies beneath like the earth does under us. When we see those who serve as lesser than those who boss around, we just encourage what we supposedly abhor. Such people as should be leaders, (in the undistorted vision of the White Realm) would be viewed as 'door mats' or 'betas' rather than 'bridges' by today's competitive culture.

In this way we discourage true leadership and even as we speak out against tyranny we reproduce it in ourselves and upon each other. The spirits of the white dragon realm have the same relationship to stars and light that faeries have to plants and trees. Thus they are in all of us, in the parts of us made of stars, which have evolved like tiny ghost lights into awareness moving through synapses. It is through our awareness that we are touched by angels or sky beings, we only need to remember how to listen to them. Though we have hijacked them and attached them to the masculine principle there is nothing universally true about this designation. There are many other possible stories that are less distorting and exhausted.

Just as science is pointing towards the existence of the need for an observer, a consciousness who sees something happening and thus makes it become, makes it manifest and take form one way rather than another, trees and stars and other natural phenomenon may be seen as either the bodies or the witnesses of other unseen bodies these spirits have. We may not be able to know for sure whether trees are dreaming faeries into being, or whether faeries are dreaming up the trees but we can touch the edges of the interplay from the perspective of the green within the self. Angels are the dreams of stars, warrior angels the dreams of electrical storms and solar storms. Or alternatively those natural phenomena are the result of their motions.

You can tell a lot about a culture by what it believes in regards to the heavens. Catholicism believed the earth was at the centre of the cosmos, we believe we are right on the edge of some random, meaningless location. Whilst our belief is literally true in regards to positioning, how we choose to phrase and attach meaning to this fact is still a matter for belief. The attachment of 'meaningless' and 'random' to the assessment of our position in the cosmos makes for a different story than if we'd used the word 'mysterious'. Meaning is given space to blossom by the word mysterious in a way it is not by random, and mythic truth always goes hand in hand with any other form of truth, no matter how dry and analytical we try to be. Mythic truth is required to nourish us and form points of connectivity between our sensory experience of the world and our intellect.

Just as Cu Chulainn desperately needed to uncover his eyes and see the bared breasts of the women so he could regain his appreciation of softness, so is the Over Culture we are still shackled to in various ways. Meaning is to be found in the instinct that drove the women to bare their breasts to him, his battle furore is the lust to consume and destroy that drives our collective body of One Flesh towards its own extinction in this current world age. It is imperative that we turn our eyes now upon the flesh gnosis those women displayed, and their healing instinct and remember that our bodies know what to do even when our minds are confused.

We cannot do this by dividing ourselves from each other with hard delineations that mark out women from men or based on skin pigmentation, for we are all part of a sliding scale of characteristics always capable of erupting with the Other, as we are part of one chaotic flesh monster with it all. We, the many-headed red beast are the stead of Babylon ... We have inside us each the resistant, stubborn Cu Chulainn and the women who know when their breasts can provoke healing, we have also a sovereignty who knows how to guide us back into Right Relation.

It is also why Cu Chulainn loved the faerie woman, Fand, and couldn't be with her lest his nature destroy the other faeries with his presence. He needed her greenish hued enchantment as desperately as his almost sterile aridity required the reddish blush of sensuality. Throughout the story his healers present themselves to him one by one, but in his pride he has not learned how to say yes to them, in fact he actively reviles that which is attempting to heal him.

Myth is how the realm of faerie (green) carries messages from the sensory realm of the body (black/red) to the intellectual realm (white). So every myth that overlaps with other myths, tells the tangled tale of a culture the faeries have a hand in. They leave clues like these, stories that can be read multiple ways ... The faeries are here reminding us that when white dragon sickness seizes an individual or culture they still desire the greenness, even after they've reviled the black/red, yet you cannot have access to one without the other. You cannot destroy what feeds the hungry root and still think you can capture the flower at the end. Such is the delusion of our current Over Culture in a nutshell.

Basque culture, possibly the closest to a purely chthonic (Underworldly) polytheism left intact in Europe, believed that the sun and the moon were brought into being in the Underworld and rested there again in their mother at night. Whilst this isn't literally true this story that makes the earth a fertile haven of the silver and golden lights of the heaven, makes us feel very differently about the earth than our modern story. As a result, this story becomes a balm that both feeds our sensuality and our need for enchantment, in listening we say yes to the healers of the red and green who appeared to offer Cu Chulainn anointment with cool myrrh and sweetening nectars. In his aloneness, like a ravening hound, he must consume his own dog flesh from the inside out.

If we are going to try to address our out of control whiteness fetish (and yes I mean this to have all possible implications) we will need to understand that whilst it might be literally true that earth came from the stars, it is more *therapeutically* true to keep telling myths that talk about how the heavenly bodies came from the earth. Let us earth a little of the pride of our star-fire-minds in the bosom of our mother, let us gaze upon the bare breasts of the women and find calm, let us say yes to the Morrigan and fuck the land rather than *fuck up* the land. Let us, like the Ancient

Mariner, gaze upon the slimy creatures of the deep, all that we've been taught should be reviled, and bless them until the albatross we carry slips from our necks.

To find again the better angels in and outside ourselves, we should begin with the moon. Lilith's lantern is both a corpse light and a leaker of softened sun-dew. She appears in the sky like a mirror image of the light within the Underworld. Her sky waters make a bridge between heaven and below ground, which consist of one water system, carrying and churning the produce of the light. The dark side of the moon, which swallows her for three days a month is when the sanguine and salty waters of the Underworld must discharge and a cessation of the incoming power from the sun must halt, is like an Underworld sister of this lunar queen of the heavens. During the dark of the moon the black bull of the abyss mounts her. She is ridden by him until the sun arrives and gradually as the sun mounts her ever deeper, the bull withdraws.

On the days where there is growing light she is beginning to lactate, progressively turning the moon white with her life dew. She lactates because the sun brings to her the mixed influence of all the other planets as a gift that he secretes inside her like begetting their child. On the full moon the queen of the heaven bursts forth with her maximum gush, as though in the throes of both orgasm and childbirth. At that time the sorcerer must go alone beneath her silver light and capture the exact moment of the moon coming to full in a glass bottle where gin, bladderwrack, camphor, lavender and pine have been steeping. When this is done, strip naked before the light of the heavens, stand bare and unashamed before the Maiden of the skies who opens the gates to the heavenly mansions of the planets. Rub over yourself the alcohol and lie in her beams upon the earth.

As though to move counter to the over-weening solar hero, let us lie down on our stomachs with face against the ground or in the foetal position. It might seem strange in a book called standing and not falling, but before we can stand we must learn to be grounded, for all of us start and end our lives lying down. If we are to approach the skies in a healthier way it is with the bleeding cycle of the moon that we must first walk. The work of this month is a course of moon-bathing for three nights.

When the next storm rages, after you have done this work go out in it and cut a vulva shape in the ground for the rain to pound in to, pour honey into the earth wound of it. Sing to the storm daimons. Strip your own clothes away if you can and lie down with your legs out around the cunt you've drawn, regardless of your physical sex. If you do these things you will feel the strong sexuality of the sky spirits. If there is somewhere you can be private by daylight, you may like to anoint yourself in alcohol steeped in more solar herbs and sunbathe until it dries on your skin. For women in particular, to go to a high place and open their legs to the warming sun can be a very powerful enticement to the sky spirits to show themselves in all their glory. You will feel, that unlike the distorted whiteness hero, they will quite like it when you bare your breasts or skin in general. It seems they love to feel their sky-waters caress the senses in the form of rain.

In conjunction with the above work, over this moon you will also benefit from daily meditation to begin to balance the powers of the four dragons in your body. The dragons can also be storied as the four horses of the apocalypse if that better suits your prior mythic framework. The apocalypse, of course, is simply uncovering, a dropping of the veil that conceals truth.

Begin in an upright position but supported and comfortable.

Empty your lungs, and begin in the belly of the black dragon, beneath the floor or ground, where the dead reside. Feel the fecund nature of the darkness, full of fertile rot that is ready to generate life. When you can't hold your breath empty any longer breathe in.

When you begin to breathe in, visualise the breath heading up your spine and turning green like a plant acquiring oxygen and unfurling towards the sun. When the 'branches' reach your head begin to transform the green colour to greenish-gold in transition through the solar colour to stellar white.

When your lungs are entirely full, 'burst' into the whiteness of the stellar sphere and the Star Folk of the white dragon. Hold your breath for as long as you can, maintaining the whiteness, thus forging out the head to make it a stronger receiver of stellar influence.

When you begin to release your breath and redden the power as it travels down the front of your body you are consciously incarnating that stellar power in your body, another Fall of Light from the heavens, the reddening of the stone as the angel of your being becomes ruddy with incarnation, as the rose upon the cross.

When your lungs are completely empty, hold your breath for as long as you can and consciously suckle on the darkness of the void, allowing things that are no longer needed to dissolve.

As you go around and around in this circular breath, think about consciously feeding each dragon force to the next. Feel the green realm drawing on the rot in the black and the white realm thrilling to the responsiveness of the green, and spilling down its radiant warmth upon the red dragon, that in turn must die and give over power to the blackness. Do any parts of the breath cycle seem harder or less interesting to you than the others? Details of how this work goes should be noted in your magical diary and the practice should be continued for a full moon.

Moon 3

Leaving the Bundle, Grasping the Fire-brand

Turn aside but for a moment. Turn aside from yourself, your self-image. Abandon the house of reflections and walk awhile in the clear air of the morning. Listen to the sound of your breath, to the sound of your body, and to the sounds of the world around you. Without your opinions the world still stands. Without your preconceptions the sky remains. Turn away for but a single hour from that with which you are familiar. Grant yourself the chance to be more free than you have been. Seek nothing more than the freedom to seek with open eyes. If you succeed in the primary acts of opposition you may never return to the world of men ...
(Andrew Chumbley)

If you are starting out alone, forging the path for others you hope will come, or even intending always to remain alone in your work, know that your path will be arduous but rewarding. If you begin instead well armed with occult training, the potential for some to be offered, or even an established tradition behind you, in some ways, things will be much easier.

However, if you identify more with the latter I will have to ask you for something, which may be harder for you than those who begin holding nothing. You will have your own experiences and opinions on the matters I'm about to discuss but the very practice requires a neutral mind frame, one willing to suspend either belief or disbelief and defer forming an opinion at the outset, a willingness to set aside preconceptions and experiment with the material. Someone who is not a beginner may have to work harder mentally for this position, but will have a better repertoire of tools at their disposal to accomplish it. Before we can even come to the place from which we will leave behind this bundle of preconceptions, we will need to practise something I call Stepping Out.

During the times when the bulk of witchcraft persecution occurred, life was a lot more socially fixed in place than it is for most Westerners today. All but the most wealthy of folk were forced into closer living conditions with others and most of people's daily and nightly life was watched by countless others. The practice of stepping out to the edge of the wild was potentially suspect behaviour in and of itself as it seemed to suggest the person had something to hide.

This might be hard to imagine today but when a group of people live close like this, something called group fetch (a concept I will expand upon later in this book) emerges between them. Like all collective states, this can be used for good or ill. Everyone whose ever tried being part of something that requires any kind of group mind knows that what happens with one person effects other people, and it becomes hard for anyone's issues to remain discrete.

When people don't understand how this principle works this is, incidentally, also the reason many modern folk get turned off group work. Because villages or tribes instinctually understand their interconnectedness in a way we often fail to, you only need to drop the idea into such a group that a certain personal behaviour their neighbour is getting up to (whether it be anal sex or witchcraft) will have negative ramifications on everyone, and you have a kind of witch hunt on your hands. So long as this kind of thinking is reserved for things that *actually do* have ramifications for the rest of the group (such as shitting in the water supply) then things are fine.

Clearly things were not fine in Europe during the witch persecutions ... People were made afraid easily for very good reasons to do with multiple generational trauma, exposure to public punitive violence, pestilence, famine, ergot poisoning, and institutionalized class and gender oppression. They had reason to be afraid, some of them more than others. Immediately before them in history is centuries of plague, warfare, Catholic versus Protestant persecutions, public burning of living human beings, and famine where you would actually witness the starvation of others while you were still a child.

We know these things about history, but how long do we stop to really *know* them and the radical difference of such a society? There are parts of the world with similar trauma patterns still today, and if you look at those societies you will find they are generally very reactive to concepts like witchcraft and social 'discipline' for difference. In fact, it might be said that the safety of sorcerers everywhere rests on a few generations of good harvests, a lack of immediate genocides and public executions, that our rationalism and civilized compassion rest entirely on this thin thread of good luck.

These people of the past held the genetic memory of a great deal of hardship that saw them there, still clinging onto life in the 1600s, one illness requiring penicillin away from their grave. Yet the only real difference between them and us is perhaps not just the level of fear we live in, as the media has moved in to partially compensate where public burnings dropped off (you can still see them along with beheadings and torture victims if you Google them, or even if your friends see fit to subject you to them on social media, and who knows what it does to the human psyche that these images can follow us into the sanctuary of our homes and no longer stay hanging at the public gallows), is that most of us no longer have our lives so closely enmeshed with those immediately around us. We don't fear contagion quite in the way we did, and yet we are not without those who claim other people's sexual relationships and what they do with their reproductive organs will affect society, the weather and how happy God is with us.

This sort of 'thinking' has not disappeared, and it won't in a hurry because it's a distortion of a reality so fundamental to our nature that it will take some time to be fully erased. It rests on something very real after all, the knowledge that your tragedy is my tragedy, that your liberation is my liberation ... This basic ecological understanding of our soul life is surely at the underpinning of mankind's most instinctual animism, and in this way it brings out both our best and our worst. The problem is not that we care what other people are doing to each other. Anyone whose ever lived in a bad part of town where people are abusing each other and their own bodies all around you knows the feeling in the air in such places. It is indisputable that the way the people around you are living affects you! If someone in a tribe is beating their partner this will affect the victim and the abuser, (for all abuse at some level constitutes abuse of self), any children who witness it and the general threat-assessment ability of the whole collective.

Yet we have had this instinct twisted by those who wished us to believe pleasure is as harmful, or perhaps more harmful, than pain. An ideology that wished us to believe that what other people did with their bodies with other consensual adults, what they did with their bodies' biochemistry with plant helpers, what they did with their own state of consciousness in the form of trance and spirit belief, somehow negatively impacted the community around them. This can lead some even to believe frankly ridiculous things such as that someone else's homosexual sex might be the cause behind dangerous hurricanes! Embedded social trauma has left many of us unable to tell the difference between the social implications of a consensual act and a non-consensual one and to confound the two.

Opinions have become linked to a form of control and power in an otherwise general feeling of powerlessness. Opinions, therefore, have become the one unchallenged god of this era. You have them, and therefore you are. You have a right to them, the airing of them is seen as more important than kindness and peace, they are the last thing no one can take from you, they define your identity and identity is the last field of control offered over our lives. You might not have a right to privacy or to opt out of the social contract with society, but you have the right to your opinions, god damn it! The modern ego is pretty much composed of what we support and oppose, a startling amount of what we hold opinions on have nothing at all to do with us, and probably impact us only in the most tangential of ways, yet we will fight for our right to tell everyone about them nonetheless. Social media seems to encourage us to do this belligerently by emboldening the uninformed to believe their opinions are equal to those who are more informed.

For the occultist who is identified as a witch (and even those who would not likely have been labelled as such during a true social breakdown panic) such behaviour is problematic, as we ourselves have always been scapegoats in a world so hungry to identify dangerous outsiders. Today we have elected new groups to serve as 'witches' and we are usually left alone. It is no longer considered freakish to step outside of the city, to cross the hedge and enter wild nature, what little of it the Industrial Revolution has left its descendants. But the state of mind that our Pre-Modern ancestors unconsciously feared from those eyes of the Outside being turned back to look upon them from outside the hedge, that state is still just as rare.

What does it mean then, to bundle up your assumptions and your cherished opinions about the world, your membership to different interest groups and ways of life, the things that the modern world tells you make you *you,* and leave them in a bundle at the hedge? Quite simply, to us, as to our forebears, this means death. Only the dead get to see with those kinds of eyes. Initiation, not the ritual that confirms it for your community but the thing itself, however you find your way to it, should give you those kinds of eyes that see with implacable clarity, or something isn't working properly.

If that idea makes you feel comfortable, if you are able to reassure yourself that you've already done this and have already removed the blinkers put upon you by society this is an immediate sign *you have not yet understood the full implications of the act.* Stepping Out isn't just about going to higher ground, or a place outside the town and casting your eyes back in, leaving your previous ways of thinking in a bundle at the hedge, it is about seeing with the eyes of one alien to this world. And as this world is constantly trying to pull us back in, the work requires constantly renewed effort.

Through an act of will and imagination one must slough off everything: nationality, gender, your mother-tongue language, your species ... until you are down to your bare bones with reality. Until you no longer have a knee-jerk identification with others who share the same gender as you, who want to create an Other out of those who don't, until you no longer assume the perspective of your nation and culture is central to world history. Only when you get down to the last ways in which that world can still manipulate your thinking, at which you accept the assumptions you barely even realise you carry from childhood, are you empowered to truly step back inside that system and make change within it.

Every skilled occultist will manage this to a deeper or less-so degree but hopefully each time they do it they discover a little more and leave a little more behind. It will feel scary if it's working. It will feel like your ability to function within the system is in peril. And it is. If you do this practice properly your very sanity will feel like it's in peril. Because we have been taught to believe that the ability to function inside an insane system is a manifestation of sanity. If you are going to walk this path alone at first, it will be very hard. Such work is not for the faint of heart. It is worth considering before you even set your intent how deep and steely is your commitment to go all the way with this. Because the dropping of the bundle it is not the kind of practice that sits well half done in someone's psyche.

It is a good thing to honestly examine your motivations for taking this step. If forging the way for others is your intention, you must be as free from the desire for self-aggrandizement as possible. For the path will level and humble you. The path will bring you to your knees. True witchcraft doesn't bring its adherents to their knees but its leaders ... You will bear responsibility; you must, yet you will never be fully in control of anything. Like everyone else, you will be balancing and it will take both skill and daring. Be prepared to accept the conditions of reality. One part of which is that most people do not at all respect the things that serve them, only those that they fear. Whilst you will know this and accept it in theory, this will never be an excuse to shift your behaviour to cultivate fear. The role of Path Forger (whether called Magister/a, Man in Black, Maid, Hand Maiden, Priest/ess or other or nothing, High Priestess or Grand Master) is the same regardless of what name it's given. If it is not driven by Love for your kin above and beyond all other laws, then it's worthless.

If you still wish to go ahead after consulting your own eyes in the mirror then take your bundle to the edge of the wilderness. I want you to imagine while you're preparing to do it, conjuring the glamour of this phantasy with all your witching fire, that everything you own is in the bundle. All your possessions, your ID cards, the title deeds to any properties you own, your childhood keepsakes, even letters from your dead grandparents, everything. On the other side of that hedge or gate you must pass is a whole other style of life you can't even fully imagine. It's an important part of the glamour you are creating that you *acknowledge your lack of knowledge.*

Outside that hedge, the life you must see as waiting for you contains your own wild self. It contains a life run by the principles of Nature and your humility is your first gift to it. Just as your first gift to an indigenous people whose culture you have no way of understanding is to admit your ignorance and place down as an offering your willingness to learn. This won't include impressing them by telling them all your own wonderful observations about magic, so that you can share your Western perspective with them. It will include your quietude. Only an empty cup can be filled.

Imagine that when you step through the hedge this other life will literally have you. There won't be warm beds and security where you're going; you must see it as this literal or the magic of it won't fully work. You must imagine that you will be living off your wits and the bonds you form with those around you. Until you've decided firstly that you would be willing to leave your modern Western life behind to take this kind of leap into the unknown, looking for your true self, then you have no business with magic. This is not the path of comfort.

When you have constructed this phantasy so strongly that you all but expect horses to erupt from the trees with elfish people of the woods riding them, you are ready to place your bundle. If the glamour your thoughts create is strong enough it won't matter what's really in the bundle. Only that you sit with the feeling of what it would be like to leave behind all those markers of your ego, not only the objects but the cherished belief patterns and long held opinions. Choose for this magic a place where you will be able to have privacy. If you don't feel assured of this it is a sign you haven't gone far enough into the wild.

Venture to where it is possible your human clothes can be stuffed into the bundle at the hedge and you can go on naked. Just like some tales of the Witch Goddess both in Wicca and the tale of Inanna, you are being stripped of the markers of selfhood as you descend to the Underworld. Here you must wash. Ideally it would be in a moon-drenched pool, deep, dark and bone-achingly cold enough to simulate your descent into the womb of making and un-being we call the Underworld.

If it is entirely impossible, take with you water from spring or wave in which you can wash beneath the moon. As you do so wash away consciously, cleanse yourself of your baptism into any faith or ideology you have previously been involved in. No value judgement of these creeds or factions is relevant here, they must merely be gone. Capitalism or Socialism can be as much a religion as Catholicism and all must be washed away. When this is done you will clean your nails in the most scrupulous way you've ever done before, both with water and an implement. After it is done you will declare (your first words spoken aloud since passing the hedge): 'May my soul be as clear of all creeds and systems as my nails are free from dirt.' Then you will sharpen them.

When this is done allow the water to dry on your body. Allow the feeling of emptiness to call to the Unseen like a vacuum of force waiting to be filled. For there is no such thing as a position to stand outside of other things, only a temporary glamour that allows us to see the truth of our predicament. Looking back with the eyes of one who has shed their skin, the world on the other side of the hedge may look very different to you. But just by having taken my advice, just by creating the poetry in your mind of inside and outside, us and them, you have already sided with something. The temporary vacuum state of shedding calls for renewal, for fertilization. Without explicitly needing to say so, just by Stepping Out, you have already taken on the perspective of the Otherworld, a spirit-eye view.

Here, if you have not done so already in your tradition or practice, you can call out to the Unseen and affirm this allegiance with the Other. However you choose to do so make it wild and real, make it come up from the depths of yourself, or don't bother calling at all. You might do this by shouting three times: 'Robin Goodfellow!' or, freed as you now are from religious fears and stigmas, you could call him devil, angel, faerie, incubus, god, monster … Whatever words stir fear and desire in you. Take the posture of one hand above your head the other under your foot. If you have truly stripped yourself bare of all other attachments and left your old self at the hedge, for the first time you will understand what this gesture really means.

If you don't believe me (and I encourage you to try for yourself) you can try leaving yourself in the stripped back state without making this second step of new allegiance. You will likely find that one of two things will happen. Either your old thought patterns will immediately reassert themselves or you will begin to feel directionless and apathetic with this void state. But if you feel the need to test it for yourself you could do the working over two sessions. You will, however, need to repeat step one a second time to cover anything that might have snuck back in during the time between. As you have had a chance to return to your home and ordinary life, not been carried away by a faerie people to live animistically in the forest, it is highly likely that many repeats of leaving the bundle could be required.

When re-entering the village, town or city after you have completed the process, you will engage with one of the most important parts of the process. At least it is crucial in relation to forming or sustaining your vision. How you bring this precious cargo back inside the hedge is crucial to survival. It is unlikely that you will have the opportunity to immediately start a community in the forest, far from everyday concerns, and so your vision must be forged of tough stuff.

Whenever anything is sloughed off in the presence of Otherworldly forces something is carried back in its place. It just so happens that the gifts that the Underworld beings seem to prefer are the broken things, the useless things that would otherwise be thrown out, because it's only when something is let go of that the hands are empty to hold a gift. It just so happens that they often prefer the broken people and the misfits that nobody else sees a use for as well.

There will be many things that as a modern Westerner you have no idea you are carrying at all. Such as the many things you believe you are entitled to. Not least of all you probably believe you are entitled to your opinion. But if we are to begin things in Right Relationship we must do so from the perspective that we were born naked and holding nothing. We were not even born entitled to the love of our parents, though it certainly is one of the most important and life-creating loves, in wild nature even that is not a given. Nothing is a given. But all is gift.

So when you come back inside the hedge you will know you have done this work deeply if you find yourself on your knees again, busily thanking everything that supports you. From the ground beneath your feet, to the sun above your head, to the clothes on your back, to the sweatshop labourers who probably made them, for the air in your lungs and the trees that made it, down to every animal and/or plant that has lost its life to uphold yours.

The soul of the sorcerer should be kept lithe and youthful in elasticity by constant pleasurable effort. If you find that some parts of you have become jaded, that your perceptions of miraculous or wonderful events have been dulled by contact with the charlatans and the deceptions of the world, or because you have seen too much, it is probably a good time to die again to that world and wake up to the world beyond the hedge. This must be done many times throughout life, for we live inside the hedge, passing as one of the crowd, we must always be vigilant that the world doesn't rub off on us. So even if you have faithfully followed the formula above, it pays to make manifest the work in the following way, to both magically confirm it and to slough off what is no longer part of who you are.

Begin by gathering together a bundle of old belongings that in some way link you to the idea of the world (not the vital living world of nature but the false world man has made), they may be images of a you that you can no longer identify with, they may be objects that were once of importance in the mind of a person you no longer are. Load them all into a bundle and tie it up. On a Saturday night, walk out to a place where the city or world of man gives way to the edge of the green. Before stepping over that edge lay your bundle at the threshold of the wild and kneel down on one knee with one hand on your head and the other under your foot.

While you are in this position, conjure up all your assumptions, all your jadedness, all the scaffolding on which you hang your perceptions of things that might blur the vision of what is truly before you, all beliefs in the limits of magic, will them to be also in the bundle. Imagine that you are in fact dying in this moment. Do a quick life review, as if you were confronted with the life you have led in the Underworld. When it is done, ask it to be in the bundle, into it put your name, your sex, your race, your sexual orientation, your political beliefs, your loves, your loyalties, your pains, your fears, even the oaths that bind you. Everything that is this current person you have been, good, bad or indifferent.

Imagine that you can't even understand English, that when

you step across the edge into the green you will be seeing with new eyes that have not gazed upon the world before. While you are doing this, dig a hole to bury your bundle. This is your votive offering to the wild.

When this work is complete and you must find your way back into the world of man, take something with you from the place of your liberation, the ground where your shackles were struck off. That object will be a symbol of your promise to live the vision of your outside-the-hedge self, to provide room for Paradise to flourish and manifest here in this world, and of its promise to you to move through and guide the hand that allows itself to be guided. You will become this daimon and decide which attachments, ideas, beliefs, and people to bring into its life that of old you may have previously committed to. Decisions made from the heart of the daimonic intelligence that moves behind you and through you is always in perfect rhythm with our true purpose.

Moon 4

Holding What You Have

What I have I hold …
(Robert Cochrane, *The Witch Laws*)

The typical trajectory of most students of magic without a teacher is to undertake experiments that attract the attention of the spirit world without having first worked out how they plan to swim in that sea once the water starts coming in. It is far better to know that your vessel can hold water before, rather than after, you find yourself the object of spirit attention. In this sense this book may have as well been called 'swimming and not drowning'. If you have worked faithfully through the past three moons you will already be beginning to attract attention. Other human practitioners as well as spirits may have already become aware of you if suitably capable ones are practising in your area.

Unless you are an established sorcerer who is doing this for a spiritual detox then I suggest you don't form new alliances with any of the spirits attracted to your work just yet, or with new people. If you have identified a weakness in the green or black realm via the breath work, you might have been led by commonsense to work on it via spending time in environments rich in that power. With forests and burial grounds being the most obvious sources of green and black dragon power and animal rich environments (including dancing people) and high places full of meditation and solitude being appropriate for red and white. If you've been seeking to address the imbalance, you may well have new spirits of one type or another speaking to you on a regular basis.

By all means be polite to them and interact, but if you are new to magic do not suggest or enter into any long-term arrangements as yet. Tell them that you would like to see them again at a certain point down the track and name that time. An exception might be if the entity is of ancestral origin and is clearly the spirit of a dead forebear you recognise after questioning and maybe even testing them. In that case you would be wise to begin laying a glass of water before a picture of said ancestor on a weekly basis. There would also be no harm in leaving a similarly small vessel of milk out once weekly for the faerie folk.

Beyond these simple things amounting to good manners you would be far better served to learn how to defend yourself from unwanted influence and discerning how to prove who is helpful and unhelpful before rushing into anything. The same can be applied to communities of humans as to bonds with spirits. Until you have at least passed through the work of this moon, you are far too ripe for having advantage taken of you for your newly activated fire.

One of the things increasingly apparent to me as I go along is just how much advantage a well-trained occultist has over your average person. There are reasons I could name, both magical and what might be termed psychological, things that have to do with having died before you die, with having very little fear left unpoked at and a certain imperviousness to trivialities, amongst other things. Luckily for the cowan (the uninitiated) the idea of using it to gain an unfair advantage for the sake of power alone becomes increasingly less interesting and unsporting to most of us … It's the other individuals that aren't in the 'most' that one needs to be cautious about, and they exist. Some of them are very good at what they do indeed.

There are also humans as well as spirits that will be keen to pump up a waning coven or magical circle by the injection of your fresh, newly awakened fire. These kinds of groups act a bit like a magical pyramid scheme and you can spot them by their over-eager desire to seduce and incorporate you, likely offering rapid initiation. Unless there is money involved (which there seldom is in witchcraft) teaching you represents a great deal of work and output, if the teacher or group seems over eager to expend this unpaid labour you might want to wonder why?

To make sure you get off on the right foot, I'm going to walk you through a spiritual blitz aimed at throwing off all adverse influences to your work. This is another reason why I have suggested you do not put too much effort into actively building up any new spirit helpers, as during the early stages of a human-spirit connection some of the measures I'm about to suggest could well scare some of them off.

For the purposes of clarity I will divide the work that needs doing during this moon into three phases. You may choose to divide the moon into three equal segments and work on each for that amount of time, or to, instead, work on them simply for as long as each requires with Physical perhaps being taken care off in one day and Social requiring three weeks, as needed.

As this work is about your thriving as well as surviving, it can be considered bolstering work on the red dragon parts of yourself.

Physical

To cleanse yourself you will need to acquire these ingredients: a white or plain beeswax candle, frankincense, egg shells, powdered angelica root, yerba mate, hyssop, pine needles, and camphor.

Set the frankincense aside for smoking out yourself and the house at the beginning of the ritual.

Grind a powder out of the eggshells, angelica root, and yerba mate, set this aside also.

Make a herb bath out of the pine needles, hyssop and a small amount of camphor.

Smoke yourself all over and proceed to carry the smoke to all the extremities of your home before zeroing in on the bathroom where you plan to wash. Light the candle and place the incense off to one side, get into the purifying water and entirely submerge yourself for a short time. You may form a prayer for purification from all adverse influences to whatever you believe in, whether that is gods, God, The Goddess, Fate or your own daimon-genius if you are not religious. You may find that after dropping your bundle, it will take some time to decide what, if anything, of your previous devotions and beliefs has carried through to still be useful to you. But most likely you will end up weaving in the parts of your old beliefs that still serve you in a conscious and calm manner.

When you get out of the bath allow the water to dry in your skin and snuff out the candle only when this is achieved. When you are dry, dust yourself down with the powder and if possible have a friend blow some on the back of your neck/lower head area. While this is happening remind yourself that you are actively taking ownership of your body and vital force, what you have you hold!

When this is accomplished and you are re-dressed in different clothes than the ones you were wearing beforehand, proceed to the boundaries of your outdoors property. This should be accomplished after nightfall to allow for privacy. If you are female or other stomp your foot down on the boundary and declare: 'what I have I hold'. If you are male you may urinate on the area to be warded, which may take a couple of goes depending on your control.

These statements of your magical will, in turn, strengthen said will the more often they are affirmed.

Social

Having affirmed and magically asserted your ownership of your body and your immediate territory you may find you're sensitized to noticing the ways in which people overrun your boundaries socially. I want you to think about the way you use your 'no' and 'yes', as well as how you use your magical word? Do you regularly affirm things about yourself that are not in line with how you truly will things to be? Do you affirm self-defeating things?

Get a piece of paper and plot a mind-map of yourself and the people you regularly interact with, or who still affect you in some way. Look at each of these relationships with a cool observer gaze. What is the exchange of energy like in this relationship? Does the other person overstep your boundaries or take more than they give? Do they use manipulative measures to get energy and attention from you that you would rather not give? Or do you do these things to others in your life? Both sides of this are equally important for creating Right Relations in your life. If you try to enter the spirit world as a human who doesn't pay their debts, doesn't honour agreements, takes only what they are given when it comes to loved ones, and doesn't practise reciprocity with kin, you aren't going to be taken seriously by any but bottom-feeding entities. In a perverse snowball effect this association with them will in turn deplete your levels of mental health, causing a downward spiral in your prospects.

So it's important to get this stuff right. You are aiming to establish equal, consensual energy exchanges with all the people in your life, that way all the future spirits in your life will know what kind of person they're dealing with. Once again, you can avoid shame by reminding yourself that if you discover a non-reciprocating pattern in yourself in one area of life or more you have just undergone a major power-up as an occultist by being self-aware and strong enough to own it. Shame only assists the parasites and helps us to become one. A small positive change is worth more than a thousand feelings of shame. So when you have this information, do something with it. Do not let your 'no' be overrun by someone else's will, but neither shall you overrun another's who you are in community with, for these are your kindred. Only from how you treat human kin shall other entities know how to expect you to behave in your alliance with them.

Spiritual

This technique should be used on a daily basis for this moon, and after this whenever it is felt necessary to remove unwholesome matter from one's self and to develop a 'thicker skin' to protect your boundaries from encroachment.

As you are breathing, sitting or standing in a comfortable position, send the breath to the red dragon inside the body, into the belly and the centre of yourself. Visualise it feeding on the breath coming down to it from the white realm and growing plumper and fatter, glowing red with power.

As it begins to expand, you see it pushing out any black flecks, or dull spots inside you, places where you feel resistance or pain. You might want to stretch physically beforehand so you can feel where these spots are more keenly. Every time you breathe in and puff out your belly, see the red dragon growing bigger and pushing this black shell of fragments out toward the surface of your skin.

The fragments form a covering on your skin; we are now going to use the red serpent inside us to stretch them out from our body like a protective cloak. See the strands of black restrictions being stretched by the heat your inner dragon is generating. You may feel at first you need to use different kinds of breath techniques of the explosive type or to dance to get this feeling of limber body heat, but eventually you will be able to perform this at will, even with your eyes open.

Stretch the fabric of your new cloak out around you, pulling it and tugging it in all directions until it is supple and mist-thin. Practise contracting it tightly until it turns black and forms a barrier between you and someone encroaching on your space; try making it feel spikey. Afterwards smooth it out again and expand it until it forms a misty cloak of invisibility.

Each day work on building your cloak and working through its different levels of density, opening it to let someone closer, closing it suddenly, practising becoming functionally invisible in public. What you are doing here is harvesting little rigid fragments of black serpent that have become broken off in your soul to turn into a cloak that works for you. Everyday that someone tries to send more of these in your direction they can be taken and harvested into more power for your cloak. But remember it is the red dragon in your belly that denatures the harm from this substance; otherwise you are just coating yourself in a poison rather than converting a poison into a medicine.

If you find yourself feeling something actively trying to push past your defences during this moon, you might like to try this. Here is the technique I use (a more defensive extension of Cloaking) when I feel like I need to clear things out after an unpleasant experience. If I've done this and worked on my cloak regularly but still experience problems, I might ask another practitioner to look over me for a second opinion.

1. Do your normal pushing outward of the Witch's Cloak to encircle yourself, by using your red serpent. But this time, heat the red serpent up to white hot until your bones glow. This can be accomplished through movement or through storing and

feeding unused sexual vitality to your fetch.

2. When you can feel that white hot centre, push it up and out through all of the orifices of your skull. This should look like a big white fire ejaculation through your face holes! But not just the mouth, nostrils etc., but also the spirit gate at the back of your head. I tend to blow out strong through my nostrils at the same time and see them being 'whooshed' clear.

3. Incorporate any burnt debris that has been expelled into the outside of your Witch Cloak, and push it much higher above your head than normal. As though you were placing a wider space between outside influences and the entrance to your head. Sit with clear thoughts and no mental chatter for a while in this state of 'holding the hood high'.

4. Smoke yourself down with things like Frankincense and St John's Wort.

Moon 5

Healing with and in Community

One day a man said to God, 'God, I would like to know what Heaven and Hell are like.'

God showed the man two doors. Inside the first one, in the middle of the room, was a large round table with a large pot of stew. It smelled delicious and made the man's mouth water, but the people sitting around the table were thin and sickly. They appeared to be famished. They were holding spoons with very long handles and each found it possible to reach into the pot of stew and take a spoonful, but because the handle was longer than their arms, they could not get the spoons back into their mouths.

The man shuddered at the sight of their misery and suffering. God said, 'You have seen Hell.'

Behind the second door, the room appeared exactly the

same. There was the large round table with the large pot of wonderful stew that made the man's mouth water. The people had the same long-handled spoons, but they were well nourished and plump, laughing and talking.

The man said, 'I don't understand.'

God smiled. 'It is simple,' he said, 'Love only requires one skill. These people learned early on to share and feed one another.'

(Traditional Fable)

No man is an island, and no occultist can be said to have established a good healthy place to work from until they have established Right Relations. This means being on good terms with as many of your immediate community of humans and non-human entities of all sorts. These are your allies for when you eventually come along things or people who wish you serious ill.

The magical home is the first step in creating a healthy meeting point and it will be much easier for you to establish yourself as a sorcerer if you aren't fighting pitched battles right from the beginning with other practitioners and entities. The path is hard enough, so why make it harder? Begin from a place of harmony and when something eventually decides to take a swipe at you, you will be standing somewhere firm.

Let us think about our house at a mythic level as the home of the witch. The cottage in the enchanted forest, overgrown, mysterious ... The Baba Yaga hut on its chicken legs ... the weird, the strange and the sinister interconnection of the outside with that which is *inside*. There are ghosts riding on the backs of the mice inside the walls of this unseen ghost of your house, lying just behind the *seen* house. The spectres of mummified cats hunt them at night. Strange spiritual middens build up of broken household objects taken by the hands of the pale folk to the subterranean realm that has its mouth in the narrow space below the floorboards.

Bones of the dead live under the stones of the hearth and goblins congregate in the devil's acre, the wild part of the yard given over for the usage of the People From Outside. In the form of the witch's house, the outside is on the inside. Such is the weird inversion of normative order that the witch, whose person embodies revolution, creates around them.

When you returned from having dropped the bundle and seizing of the wild fire from the woods, you will have returned with relics filled with the virtue of your achievement. Candle wax, water from where you bathed, the ashes of a fire you might have lit, you fingernail parings from where you cleaned and sharpened your nails, some sticks and stones, these will all have become powerful talismans, marked with the fire of your vision ... Bundle these up and retain them.

For now, you must bring your vision back and anchor it in a physical location, which is also at once a community. For the first thing that must happen when the perspective of the Otherwise is known (or perhaps it's better to say when it knows you) is that the witchery of the outside must be brought back. Homes must become a little bit of the outside on the inside of the hedge. Uncanny toad-haunted places where the rules are set up differently than in other homes, for prodigies can occur there that do not happen in other homes.

Ideally, there would be a place below your floorboards or inside the walls, even better under your hearth where you could create a midden of these relics. But failing this, a spirit house can be constructed out of the twigs and the vessel filled with offerings. When you do this you are beginning the process of carving a pathway between your home and the Otherwise, so pick the location in the home accordingly. It will be more powerful if it's concealed, or if it's partly revealed and partly concealed by being visible but mistaken for an everyday object. For now this is all you will do. It would also be ideal if you can dig it back up, open it back up, or otherwise get at it occasionally.

If all else fails and your home is free from hidden nooks and crannies and you don't have a hearth with a chimney where you can hide things inside or any removable brickwork, then you may need to resort to a place outside. Constructing an outdoors fire pit can be ideal because by burying objects underneath, you will have regular access to adding to the pit, furthermore, the act of lighting a fire over the top from time to time will help to enliven and empower the doorway you are creating.

If you decide you will go with this option you will need to dig a small trench, preferably vaguely square in shape and line it with feathers, leaves, ash etc. from your place in the wild where you surrendered what was between your hands. You may also like to bury some offerings that will entice the spirits, such as eggs (whole), honey and milk, maybe a splash of some whiskey or rum. They should be hens' eggs. These offerings are the produce of the world inside the hedge, being offered to what is without, which is symbolized by the lining of the offering pit. When this is done cover over what you've left with more ash, leaves or feathers and cover the hole over. If you have been making offerings to the fae, you will now move these to this location.

On top of this, you will want to construct a small fireplace in a circular shape with rocks but we will not be lighting the first fire here yet until we have established the home as a witch's house from the ground up. This is where we take the things we've seen and learned from the Outside and make them part of our everyday life. When it comes to including others in your practice, it will be crucial that you get these first stages right. Think of them as the much-ignored flagstones in the temple floor, with the temple you are trying to build being the magically enlivened home.

The first thing you will want to establish is Right Relations with those beings who fall within the boundary fences of the property. You might notice I say *the* property, not your property. It will also help if you make a point, right from the start, of no longer referring to it as 'your' property, or any of the animals or plants that live there as your possessions. Whilst you will still need to retain them to function in everyday society, the habit of mind involved in this needs to go first before Right Relations can be established. Let's talk a bit first about what I mean by this term before we go any further.

'Right Relations' refers to one's perspective as underpinned by animism. That is, as you view everything as possessing some level of soul and identity, things cannot simply be treated as things, explicitly living things even less so. As our society tends to reject slavery (whilst continuing to exploit covert forms of it …) we already understand that one cannot own a person. So to think animistically, we only need to extend personhood to the other entities around us and things will begin to fall into place. If you choose to include a living thing in your household it will make plain to you the next stage in expanding the ecology of our thinking: we are connected.

So the way you extend respect to those living things around you, whether human, animal, plant or the unseen denizens of your environment is how you extend and also *create* self-respect. How you treat them is not just how you would like to be treated as many mainstream religions say, but *actually* how you are treating yourself. Every single relationship within the threads that hold together your dwelling is connected to every other. There is no holding other beings in slavery without also holding one's self less free. For slavery makes an assault on the dignity of all life, the dignity of which is to be found in its capacity for freedom to explore and unravel its own inner purpose.

Now you may be beginning to apply this to everything you eat, wear and do, and if you do you will probably be feeling despair if you're truly thorough about your assessment. Just giving up meat and animal products won't free you from this moral burden, as an animist you will begin to realise that the wood you use for paper and the plants you eat are just as real persons and just as enslaved. I'm not saying that boycotting certain products, animal or otherwise is not one correct response to the realisation of our interconnectedness, merely that the most powerful starting point is what is immediately around you.

As you gain power and increased ability to enact your worldview around the home, from there you can ripple out and try to change the way the modern world forces you into systems that support slavery. So let us put the rest of the world outside the boundaries of your home to one side for now, to return to later. This is just good strategic sense, and a good occultist must familiarize themselves with long-range strategic thinking. Too often we lose all our impetus, frittering it away on battering against an impossible sized enemy before we've even taking the first step of enacting the principles in our own life.

There are three main types of relationships in Nature, co-operative ones, predatory ones and avoidance ones. You will still have all of these kinds of relationships with other living things, including sometimes other humans, if you are to survive in this world. But if you want to be on friendly terms with certain entities you are going to want to be in a co-operative relationship. The natural law of all non-predatory arrangements in Nature is reciprocation. The extreme of non-reciprocation is slavery with many sliding scales of predation. Predation is of course also a natural law. But when predatory relations are present inside communities of creatures there is something else less productive going on.

To begin with, the ground beneath your home was disturbed to build your property, most likely without offerings or right compensation paid to the gnomic and Underworldly spirits below. Begin the process of rectification from the ground up, literally. You will probably also need to offer to the green kingdom because it's most likely that trees and plants were also destroyed in the process. Divination with pendulum is often a great method of discovering what type of offering might be satisfactory. But simply beginning to make daily offerings to these entities, regardless, is a great place to start. Remember, as a human occupying this place you are already likely 'in the red' to these creatures, so starting off making offerings for some time before asking for anything, even an appearance or sign of their presence or interest, would be advisable.

Then consider the green people you share your environment with. Are there any of their folk who you don't use to live on that you could set free from captivity with fair belief they could live in the wild outside of pots? Are there any that don't really need to be pruned so heavily? If you must kill them to eat, honour them to the same degree you might if you killed a chicken to eat. Plants like to be informed their time is coming beforehand so they can allocate their nutriment to others of their kind. If you need to, take some non toxic material like red clay or charcoal and fat and draw distinctive human faces on all your trees to remind you daily that you are watched by the subtle minds of an alien species at all times. Treat every green thing in the house with the same regard you would an animal. Only after you have managed this leap of thinking should you begin to make offerings of milk and honey to the faeries of this realm. They won't be able to view you as a real person either until you can reciprocate by seeing their realm as sentient.

When you have, as best you can, restored dignity and personhood to the other-than-human beings with whom you share your immediate environment, you will need to turn your attention to your human connections. So let's start with the people that you share your home with, if any. If someone were to do an energy audit on your household in regards to the other occupants would you be in the red or in the black with these people? Do you hold any conscious or subconscious opinions (visible by your actions) that you've been taught by the Over

Culture meaning you are entitled to more of someone else's effort than is fair or even? This will have been so normalized for you it might be hard to see at first. You will have been taught whether you're a business owner or a worker, that it is fair and natural for one person to make a great deal of money and the other to make very little and be expendable to the business. This mindset can carry over into other parts of life where the person who is used to being a 'boss' will assume the same privileges in other parts of life, or the person who is a worker for someone will assume the right of people like their boss to live off other people's labour. Regardless of what you think politically of our economic system, these are still unexamined assumptions that are better off examined.

Here you must be especially brutal with yourself, because any tendencies like this will be amplified the moment you come into the possession of power, which properly practised sorcery will yield you. People who have been on the less privileged end of the scale need to watch themselves too, because there is nothing more likely to produce a bully than power suddenly handed to someone who has traditionally been kept down. Those who find themselves likely to just sit back and let others carry part of their load unless told otherwise will usually let people fawn on and serve them. If you wish to hold a light up for others you must make sure your conscience is entirely clear of shirking. If you are not reciprocating fairly with someone, you are no longer in Right Relation with them.

This is to protect yourself as well as others and create a stable home environment in which your magic can grow. Resentment will soon creep in as the beginnings of that person's self-protection instincts and the quality of life and vitality in your home will diminish if this kind of injustice goes on too long. So take this work seriously, take down a list of what you bring to those around you and what you take. Be inclined to be generous with your estimation of others and harsher on yourself, this will make up for your cognitive biases in your own favour and make you a better occultist and maybe teacher later on. Your home will rise or fall on the basis of your ability to do this kind of self-audit.

Earlier we have said that nothing is a given, all is gift. This is the mindset of the hunter or the warrior-sorcerer, a mindset we are wise to cultivate. This is what it means to sharpen your claws. Resurrect a live vigilance in an era of vacant staring without noticing. Expecting nothing in particular but open and alert is a fabulously powerful way of mind, leaving you prepared for anything. Whilst nothing is a given, and all things should be treated as a gift, even reciprocation, this does not change the fact that there is such a thing as Right Relations. This is determined by Nature, not by man, it is Grandmother Weaver who gets to decide and reciprocation is the law of the Old Woman. This truth is manifest via practical signals, in that most entities don't want to continue to deal with someone who doesn't reciprocate.

If someone falls out of Right Relations with you it is wholly sensible to cut off free access to your physical and emotional resources to this person, after fair attempts have been made to encourage restitution and it has been resisted. This does not constitute an expectation, it is never a *given* that other beings will stay in balance with you, when they do, receive it as a gift for in this way your joy will be more. When they do not, let them know it and ask them to restore fairness, if they will not then try another being until one does, rather than seeing one as representative of the whole. This encourages lazy thinking and bitterness that does little to improve the character or cunning, as it cuts off our awareness of opportunities presented to us if we are too jaded to see them.

In this way one's mind is kept clear and open to noticing useful anomalies in the system around us. This is how you find the Others. *They are the ones ready to meet you gently and firmly in Right Relation.* This is how you will find them, but to know this of them, they must be tested. Before someone can be tested they must be given opportunities, and you can't give a true opportunity without risking a little trust investment here and there. A hunter may miss many times and still eventually bring home the kill with persistence, and be resilient enough to bear the disappointments. So will it be for you. If you let bitterness take over your heart early on then you will still have missed and also come home empty handed.

Equality of all persons from the ground up means a vision of total reciprocity; so do not settle for anything less from the get-go. You need to be capable of at least setting this tone in your immediate environment before you can reproduce it in a coven or magical fraternity of any kind, or before you can judge the right sort to join. Such a person who is out of kilter with their immediate and nearest will not be able to model right relations for new-comers.

Of course, the fact we are out of balance with the Old Woman Herself as a species is another matter entirely and probably the reason we are so often unconscious of unequal exchanges or unable to tell the difference between abusive and non-abusive differences in people's behaviour.

I would like to speak now to the seeker who finds himself or herself upon the doorstep of a teacher, or even a coven or lodge and is considering entry. My perspective comes from witchcraft and so I will address the subject using this terminology, but what I have to say here is applicable to other paths. To the one who has stumbled to the door of the witch's house and is not the path-forger through the forest, but has followed whatever fateful trail of crumbs has led them there, congratulations. If the person you've discovered is everything they purport to be then your journey will be greatly streamlined.

Do not expect that these people will always make you feel comfortable. Only worry if they make you feel *unsafe,* being comfortable and being safe are not the same thing. This is a difficult ask for any seeker to negotiate and your canniness and your courage here both are crucial, as it is just as risky to invest in a human-to-human magical interaction as it is to trust an unproven spirit. People who have truly cast off their own bundle and brought back Fire should unsettle you because they should be Other, but you should not be afraid of them. They should make you feel unstable, uncertain, at times, but not threatened.

Your heart must make compact with theirs before the productiveness of that discomfort can be harvested. You alone know it, your heart of hearts, in the wise-beast that lives in your innards whether the feeling of strong arousal, or holy dread, that may come upon you at times in the presence of those who embody revolution, is a sign that you fear for your safety or only for the safety of the coddled notions about life you have held dear. It may turn out that you are not willing to surrender those notions, that you love them dearer than the path ahead. And such it must be for some people. This path requires both great flexibility and steely resolve and some seem destined to walk it alone. It is not for everyone to work magic in a group. But if it is for you, you will know it in the presence of those who embody it.

In speaking to the seeker, I am also speaking to those who would teach. Much can be gleaned about how to teach and pass on a Craft that you might already possess from observing my advice to students. You above all others must be hard on yourself and your motives and your integrity. Teaching and path-forging are the hardest way of all and will leave even less room for self-sentimentality than is open to students. But sometimes it's only in teaching that we work out how to truly learn. Here I will share what I've learned from watching my elders.

A witch won't just give you her magic and her secrets; they have to be seduced from her at the right time, with the right questions. A witch won't answer too soon or the too abrupt questions, but he will take note of which ones you asked and ponder why. Though she will be stretching you, she will not be testing you. That she has done already, far before you realised. The witch skilled in the Art will gently stretch you in every direction, feeling out where you give and where you resist, before applying any pressure – for teaching is healing by another name. If you want to learn from him pay attention to everything, to the way he sets out his home and the meaning of common seeming objects. When the moment feels right, ask questions about the things you notice, but don't assume they are just common things or that because you've heard about them once you know all there is to know of them. There are stories upon stories to be unpacked there.

Always ask a witch the silly questions, you may find she values your vulnerability more than your cleverness. Is that little jar just a pot or a spirit vessel? Why does it look like that and why do you place it there? If you want to learn from a witch, you need to learn from the idiosyncrasies of her Craft, for there the reddened richness runs deepest. After all, Fate sent you to this witch, not to another.

Do not touch things in a witch's home without asking, for you never know what spirit hides in a common seeming object or what was not placed there by accident. Above all pay attention. And when you think you've become good at paying attention, pay more attention. Practise noticing the way in which you listen, and when others have begun to breathe differently. When you're around a witch try to be quiet enough to sometimes hear them breathing and to enter silence with them.

A witch skilled in the Art will have hidden the magic under the tea cozy and next to the knives and forks and inside the most secret recesses of her home and heart. But every secret will only unlock for you to the extent that your own heart comes unravelled in the secret's hands. If it stays locked shut, the secret will remain a commonplace thing to you, hidden in plain sight, right before your eyes, and unmarvellous even when revealed.

Remember as you enter that what you are entering may well

be a fully developed culture in its own right, not just a subculture. Treat it with the respect you would any other foreign culture. Look for its internal logic before judging it by a foreign code of values. And do it the respect of testing its mettle first before initiation rather than seeing initiation as your chance to test what they've really got ... An initiation taken with false intentions in the heart will never yield to you the true value of that tradition, you may go away claiming it was false when indeed *you were*. If you are still thinking about veracity and judging their worthiness to have you in their group then you aren't ready to be adopted into a family with these people. Perhaps your blood family hasn't respected you and so it's hard to understand the matters of honour and loyalty that adoption and kinship should entail. If you know this about yourself, these are things to bring up during your apprenticeship as soon as you are aware of them. These are things that working through this book should help to flush out.

People who've been part of a developed culture for some time may sometimes forget that what brotherhood means to us is not always clear to those who've never truly had a brother or a sister. For many of us, true kinship will need to be relearned from the ground up. If the tradition you are considering is of any power or stature at the point you come inside, you will find there a coherent and idiosyncratic worldview, after a year or so you may see things you didn't see at first, by three you certainly will. Witches view things slant-wise to how anyone you've ever encountered before does things, and to some extent this will be the case for all decently powerful occult paths. They won't sound like just everyone talking about the topic on social media, they've come from a different world in some way. Otherwise if you don't find that, you may as well just stay on the Internet.

There is something a little different about them and it should be unnerving at times, but not purposely intimidating. If you do not feel these things, either the sense of a developed culture and coherent worldview, and even faintly unnerved, there is a good chance you are entering a House in its infancy. This might be all right for you if you are someone who likes to be involved in moving something forward, but may not work for you if you're the more receptive type who needs strong guidance. Powerful witches are unnerving because they give off a sense of relaxed alertness. Many read such people as a threat, because in our world of virtual somnambulism their very presence of mind and alertness to their environment is a systemic anomaly. When it's working on autopilot, our mind seeks anomalies in our world to pick out potential threats.

What you need to worry about is if it is not a relaxed form of alertness in the group but a sense of regular fight-or-flight behaviour. If the coven is tense and nervous around a leader of some kind (and I don't just mean the honest and obvious type of leader who has a name for their office but the unofficial populist that everyone listens to but who says they aren't leaders as well) and are super quick to see a potential threat in everyday situations, this should concern you. If you want to be part of an existing tradition but can't see an opportunity for this, do remember you're now a sorcerer. If you have the nerve, the priorities, and your beacon light has come on, someone tends to find you. The things I've said here aim to make sure the *right kind* of person finds you first.

Getting back into Right Relation with the bigger picture system outside our home is a matter that's downright revolutionary in scope and will be no small matter. Much of that battle is taken out of our hands in various ways by the way our society is organised and policed, but we can still make improvements, and maybe more. As this book progresses, we will at least begin to work through some early steps in that process. But for now, what is important is that we enact what we have been taught, otherwise we will get bogged down in critiquing the system and not start with ourselves. Only through action do we truly make a new teaching a part of us and formulate further strategies. It is one thing to say we understand that what is taken is truly given and that what is given is truly taken. That we are the other, and that when we take advantage, when we manipulate or force others into relations with us that are disadvantageous to them and advantageous to us, we are participating in the thought pattern, if not the actuality of slavery.

You will not be able to tell yourself enough times that you cannot have happiness in community whilst one is being oppressed as you are lifted up. No one is free until you all are. This doesn't mean you have to agree with other people's lifestyles or views; you just have to accept that they have the same requirements as you for life and you may need to work with them. That doesn't give you the right to assert how they ought to live.

You may have to feel the consequences of wrong action and then you will have to feel what it's like to replace it with right action. Pride grows up like a hardy plant in the cracks that change leaves behind in the hardened places in us. Pride is the first of our new allies that will help to give us power to move inside the hedge whilst the eyes of the world gaze upon us daily in judgement because our freedom makes the world uncomfortable.

Pride doesn't feel like a cloak you wear against the evil eye of a world who will often scorn you for being Otherwise. Pride is more like a fire in the belly that comes from carrying truth that ignorant words can never touch, and from walking your talk. When you know you walk your talk, in fact, maybe even walk a bit more than you talk, you won't have to worry about trying to get the respect of others, because you'll have it for yourself, and then others will tend to throw it at you whether you need it or not.

You can't get that without the contented sense of self-respect that comes from being in Right Relationship with those around you. If you don't believe me, try it. And when you have felt the psychic relief of it at a small scale, you might like to stop and consider all the aspects of survival where you are forced to rely on a faceless system, which you were never asked if you wanted to be part of; how you have never learned the skills that would have allowed you Right Relationship with the large ecosystem outside the fences on the property you live on. Generally only indigenous people in some remote areas are still able to understand that even deeper level of self-respect that comes of knowing you live in balance with all and aren't in the red to any power or creature. Understanding this will give you an insight into the invisible stressors the primitive parts of your self are living under every day.

But never fear, you had ancestors who did have access to that level of self-respect, and as the dead are never absent from the marrow of all living, what they had you also contain. This cannot be taken from you. This is land that can't be stolen, this is gods that can't be outlawed, this is old ways that can't be forgotten or tainted or poisoned or forbidden. This is blood and the holy thing passed down in love and the black heart of mystery that pulses beneath it. This is perhaps the most revolutionary thing in the whole world and it's very much alive inside you. You just need to knock at its door. Their pride is your pride, for you are your ancestors walking, all the way back to the ancient ancestors shared by every living human. *Nothing has been taken that can't be taken back.*

Here is a method our sodality uses to diffuse or transmute problems as they arise in the group consciousness. This can be very usefully applied when black serpent dominant energy (rage, fear, control, jealousy, resentment etc.) is coming to the surface in relation to sex.

Point of dispute or problem arises:

1. Does this thing harm the group or me directly?

If the answer is no, take a deep breath and walk it off. Later when emotions are less high consider what your reaction says about where you're at? What did you feel you needed to defend? When someone else was doing it differently to you, what did you feel? Acknowledging when we are threatened by difference can be much more empowering than becoming overtly defensive.

If the answer is yes and they are a member of your spiritual community, discuss your upset with them in as straight forward but caring terms as you can. Explain why it hurts you directly.

If they are outside your community, stop and think. Decide how important the damage they are doing to you/your cause is versus the damage that will be done to future relations by shooting your mouth off. If the harm they are doing to you or your cause is significant enough, engage them how you see fit.

2. Does this problem/dispute revolve around something that doesn't exactly hurt anyone, but you think could be handled better?

Many of us believe we can do things better, but do you have an alternative solution? If we're going to criticize, let's step up with a better way. Encouraging a culture of never knocking down unless you have something to put in its place is really helpful. If the answer is yes, you do have an alternative idea, suggest it respectfully. Remember, you and the other person are working for the same thing and it's always better if we don't see our way of doing things as a symbol of our self-worth, i.e. becoming married to your idea.

3. Does this problem/dispute etc. cause harm to people outside my immediate community?

This one is a tricky area because it veers perilously close to minding other people's business for them, which is often a big problem in community. This one will have to be left up to each individual to decide how they deal with their perception of harm in regards to other sovereign adults. Certainly, if a sensible law is being broken, such as one there to protect children or other vulnerable people, this behaviour should be reported. If it's a matter of social justice such as cultural appropriation, perhaps consider reporting the matter to the relevant community to see how they would like to deal with it rather than assuming you know on their behalf.

It is quite possible that there will be aspects of the lives of your spiritual community members that you don't really need to have any opinion on one way or the other... I know this is radical in this day and age where we think therefore we opinion, but it is a lie that other people's sexual lives need our monitoring or attention. This power is only destructive when it has been shamed and malformed. If we're going to work towards unravelling that damage then we mustn't reinforce shaming within our own communities.

If the answer to all three questions about harm is 'no' then the thing is probably not really a problem, but has touched off a reaction in you, an aversion or taboo. As such, you may gain power from direct confrontation with that taboo. That is how we all grow in community by looking at why we react to something. If you're hoping to successfully navigate a close-knit spiritual community then you will do best to have a relatively forgiving approach to how many things you think are your business and require an opinion/judgement from you. I have found the 'is this thing actually harming me or my cause or does it just make me uncomfortable for some other reason?' question to be an invaluable tool.

Of course, the question of getting into right relationship with the animal realm is bigger than just forgiving ourselves for being animal. Though it's fair to say that in this case healing, like charity, begins at home, we must also look at our attitudes towards other animals. We have spoken already about the importance of letting go of the belief that our very specifically defined type of intelligence makes us so much better than other animals already. But of course there are all kinds of painful implications of this sort of thinking. Some people try to resolve this issue for themselves at least by no longer consuming animal products. Whilst this may go some way towards addressing the industrial scale cruelty of the mainstream meat industry, the attitude alone only merely allows animals access to equal footing with man, whilst needing (to avoid starvation) to deny it to other life forms.

At some point we have to confront the fact that some degree of predatory relationship must occur with other life forces, and how do we reconcile that with recognition of their personhood. Our forebears seem to have used ritual to fulfil the same function that we discussed above with BDSM – taking an impulse that begins in the predatory centre of the brain and converting it into an act of sacrifice, followed by appreciation and the oneness activity of eating. In the culture of a people in Right Relationship with the rest of the animal kingdom, we die with the animal, we celebrate its essence and we become one with it in eating, letting it dance through us, taking its strengths and powers into ourselves to live on. The animal is loved for the pleasure and succour it gives with its flesh, fur, horns, blood and bone, not dominated brutishly or with industrial efficiency.

As you can see, getting back into Right Relationship with the animal kingdom *as well as the green realm* would be no mean feat in this society. Each of us can only do our best within our Fate-given means, and struggle with all our sorcerous and practical might to get free of unhealthy relationships with other life. Because when it comes to the spirit world, debts are eventually called in.

Here are some more troubleshooting tips for keeping the peace in community:

1) If you are forming a conflict with another person, use

it as an opportunity to see some things about yourself. Does this person's behaviour remind you of something you painfully repress in yourself? Perhaps they are extraverted and confident and you have bitten your tongue and stepped back your whole life? Is this tension telling you there is something you've not allowed in yourself? Is it, perhaps, whatever inhibits you from being more like that which you are angry at, rather than this person?

2) Has this person drawn attention to an area of insecurity or shame you were carrying? Perhaps you will notice you have a pattern of over-defending yourself when someone tries to discuss something with you where you are inclined to over-react?

3) Does the person remind you of yourself and things about you that you're ashamed of and find very dislikeable when they are mirrored in another? Or perhaps a behaviour that you very recently threw off and are trying to keep off? What is it about those behaviours that are so unlikeable when projected by another?

4) How much are you still resting on expectation that your wishes all be known and fulfilled by others? Are you giving sufficient respect to the Otherness of the other? Considering that their life's purpose is not to give you everything you expect, nor is it your life's purpose to twist yourself around to please someone else. Do you engage in subtle punishing behaviours towards your loved ones when they don't succeed in doing everything you want them to?

5) Are you still having problems asserting your 'no' but

feel too ashamed to admit before others that you haven't stood up for yourself yet?

6) Is there someone or more than one person in your life projecting these kinds of things onto you? Are you conscious of being someone else's shadowy mother figure or judgemental father, mean ex, or other projection that has nothing to do with your real personality? In short, of not being seen by them because they are so locked in their own wants and needs and internal projections of shame and guilt?

7) Do you care what others think of you to the extent that it could be used to manipulate you? Either through desire for social approval or fear of repudiation, can people control you to act a certain way? Do you show off to glean the approval of people you perceive as powerful, seeking their approval and feeling shame if they disapprove?

8) When you read these, do you find it initially very easy to see them in all your friends instead of applying them to yourself? Or do you apply all of them to yourself and feel personally attacked by the list?

If any or all of these things apply to you, congratulations, you're still human!

You also have lots of fruitful ideas for growth areas. You might find yourself reassessing how well you feel you were at leaving your Bundle behind at the hedge? Doing this close analysis of your patterns in relationships is like that. There is so much that we miss in ourselves until we enter into relationships and see ourselves reflected in the Other. This is why I believe personally that the right sort of group coven or lodge based magic can be very powerful and transformative.

Spend this month seeing a counsellor if this brings things up for you that you need to talk over. Even if you have good friends to go to, this is a great move in conquering shame by asking for help. It also allows you to consult a truly impartial person trained in how to listen. It is best, unless you are already aware of experiencing ongoing struggles with mental health, to make this a short-term activity, as our aim is to prepare ourselves for the magic, not to get lost in permanent navel-gazing. A lot of what passes as magical work in some quarters is little more than advanced self-help with visualisation. The idea of this book is to give people a chance to tackle all that once and for all and prepare the way. Even a simple sort of practice is infinitely more effective when moving through a prepared vessel.

Once you've done this month of work you may find that many of your relationships are actually pretty toxic. You will have to decide what to do with that information, but I assure you, any move you make in the direction of fixing your own contribution to the problem will have a 'kill or cure' effect on the whole. People who are abusers or advantage-takers of some kind seldom stick around someone finding their power. Even non-equal contributors with no intention of changing will usually bail out of a relationship the moment they are called to reciprocate equally by someone truly determined to stand their ground.

If you do wish to save a connection where you can see a lot of these behaviours in your community member, you are going to have to take the lead and be the bigger person by eliminating your contribution to the problem. Perhaps the person is passive aggressive and you always feed in the same way by asking what is wrong? Perhaps when they refuse to tell you and just keep slamming cupboards you always get angry and storm out? This time, try something different; try every different thing you can think of. Pretend not to notice, continue to be warm to them with stubborn refusal to be drawn in, confront them calmly and ask them what they hope to achieve by slamming things and not speaking.

If the problem is lack of reciprocation, stopping your contribution to the problem may be quite the opposite of patience and may require you to run out of patience and put the foot down. You may need to refuse to do something for them you would usually do, and explain why. This will require difficult conversations and probably some drama in the initial phase, but if you're honest with yourself in relationships that exhibit the above traits there has always been a kind of low-lying, minor infection, cyclically reoccurring sort of drama, hasn't there? This is just the Band-Aid-off-quick solution.

All of this becomes extra important if you are working magic with, or thinking of working magic with this person or people. As shadow-wars (where people project their traits they consider undesirable onto someone else and attack them as a scapegoat) can be souped up under the influence of witchcraft to terrifying degrees that end up doing more harm than good. Established covens can usually weather these storms better than newer ones and have methods of dealing with them and even using them to the advantage of the students' training. But for a group of inexperienced people together it is all too easy for actual witches to go on a witch-hunt among their own if they don't work through these simple but incredibly demanding stages first.

Moon Six

Healing with Place

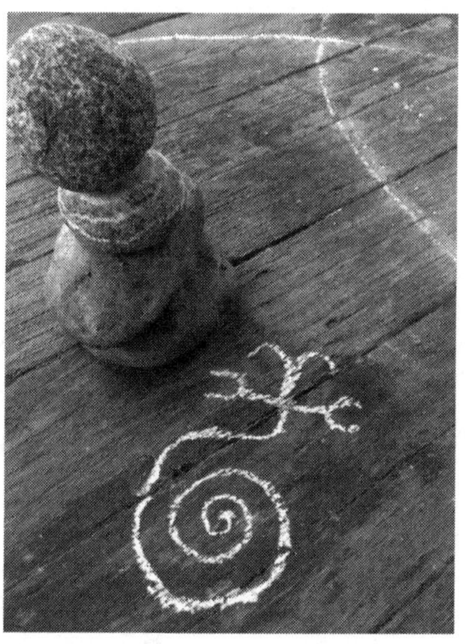

As much as I believed I was fully present in the physical worlds I was traveling through, I understood over time that I was not. More often I was only thinking about the place I was in. Initially awed by an event, the screech of a gray fox in the night woods, say, or the surfacing of a large whale, I too often moved straight to analysis. On occasion I would become so wedded to my thoughts, to some cascade of ideas, that I actually lost touch with the details that my body was still gathering from a place ...

Many people have written about how, generally speaking, indigenous people seem to pick up more information traversing a landscape than an outsider, someone from a culture that no longer highly values physical intimacy with a place, that regards this sort of sensitivity as a 'primitive'

> attribute, something a visitor from an 'advanced' culture would be comfortable believing he had actually outgrown. Such a dismissive view, as I have come to understand it, ignores the great intangible value that achieving physical intimacy with a place might provide. I'm inclined to point out to someone who condescends to such a desire for intimacy, although it might seem rude, that it is not possible for human beings to outgrow loneliness. Nor can someone from a culture that condescends to nature easily escape the haunting thought that one's life is meaningless.
> (Barry Lopez)

If there is one vastly underestimated cause for depression in our society it is the disconnection between most people and the land they inhabit. The fact we come to the table as partly disinherited is true for all of us participating in the Over Culture no matter how lucky we've been, even if we were born into a place our ancestors had inhabited since the last Ice Age, as my mother was.

I think I have become so acutely aware of this important factor because of my own personal history. As I mentioned above, my mother's family has inhabited the area broadly known as Wessex, the South-West of England (along what we call the distaff line, that science discusses in terms of mitochondrial DNA) since there was a land bridge partially open between Britain and the continent. My grandmother always said our family had been there 'forever', but the wonder of modern genetic science has confirmed this for our family in added detail. My mother was the first of that line of foremothers to leave her place and I was the first to be born outside it in all those thousands of years.

Growing up as I looked around me, first at the newly developed flat, urban desert and later at the dry, greyish-green bush, I was aware of a strange ache, a disconnect. Something deep and instinctual in my fetch knew there were meant to be stories meshing me to the landscape. When I was told the local

Dharawal people's stories about the locations around me, I happened to also know many of them were near massacre sites where people, (not my ancestors but people with the same lack of skin pigment as myself) had driven their forebears over cliffs to their death. It would be an understatement to say I didn't feel entitled to their stories or the cultural meaning encoded in them.

The landscape remained for me, faceless, strange. I felt sad when I saw people cut down its trees or dam its rivers, but it was a dull, far off discomfort. Not like when I saw they meant to frack near Glastonbury Well in Somerset! When I heard that something went through my insides like whiplash, I was entirely ready to be arrested, I just had to get back home so I could do something! Whenever I thought of it I experienced a sensation like someone had punched me in the stomach. I couldn't explain it rationally but the thought of this action was desecrating me from the inside out.

It was only back in my mother's homeland where my earliest memories derive where I was able to start putting words to what was missing. The land there had features relating to my ancestors' history, my forebears had done this, that or the other on this spot, and this was their ancient dead's burial mound, and here the devil left his toenails on the beach (fossils), in another place the faeries dance so don't go up there at night. Though it was clear much was lost thanks to hundreds of years of industrialization and rationalism, I still knew how to talk to this land, and it to me. Quickly it would forgive me for going away.

Picking up any folklore collected from minority Western cultures separated by language from those around them like Wales, Scotland, Ireland or the Basque province, for instance, will immediately reveal how much is still known. Up until the dawn of the twentieth century, and in some cases beyond, my British forebears were in possession of a rich tapestry of stories that linked them with their local landscape and its wells, cwms, mountains, lochs, menhirs, and burial mounds. Even though they also knew the stories in the Bible, this proliferation of ongoing story-making and landscape-narrative weaving is a sign that the animistic life of those populations was alive and well. New folklore arose over time without anyone needing to become self-conscious about it and whether or not it should be added to the corpus. When a tradition is robust this tends to be the case that it exhibits elasticity in including new branching tales.

But what is behind that ache of absence, of what my paternal Welsh ancestors would have called 'hiraeth,' or longing for a lost home, wasn't simply reclaimable through researching and enacting the folklore of my ancestors. Those of us now located in colonised territory such as Australia or the Americas are the descendants of the disinherited who themselves became part of the disinheritance of others. If like me you live on stolen territory never ceded, or territory that was ceded under duress or trickery, it is likely you feel the eyes of the dispossessed emanating from the fabric of Nature Herself. The story of the land you live upon must be faced and known unflinchingly, you cannot know the place otherwise.

How you respond to that knowledge in daily life, in political terms, will be up to you, but I am not here to talk people through that. I am interesting in a kind of healing that happens wordlessly, between you and a place, where you are not answerable to any human eyes, where you needn't 'virtue signal' anyone. What is going to matter here, at a magical level, is what the spirits of Place think of you. I have said already that how you treat the living who are closest to you will emanate out to the beings of the Otherness, but there is more to the story than that.

As I have been encouraging throughout this book, we need to step outside of our socially conditioned human thinking and really look at the land outside of the identity given to it by humans. I want to re-emphasis from the start that this does not free anyone from the need to engage in restorative justice towards other humans or wronged human communities as a whole. But here in the world of magic we are working from the inside out. The realm of magic has its own laws. We will need to keep one foot on either side of the hedge and be capable of stepping into the world of man to do what we think is right or getting what we need, but also of stepping out again without carrying back new mental baggage.

When we look at a land through a human-centric or anthropocentric lens we are inclined to see a land that possesses an identity constructed by the stories of whatever culture of Homo sapiens dwells or dwelt upon it. At a social level this is normal human behaviour and perfectly valid, but when we shift context, when we engage Place as a colossal non-human entity we start to realise that in this particular context such thinking cannot fully envelope this being's *sense of itself.*

It was the practice of Stepping Out that allowed me to hear the soul song of Tasmania/Van Diemen's Land/Trowenna for the first time. I had to not only shed my whiteness, but my humanity, my ability to use language or to know history ... And genuinely inhabit the eternal moment, just as the land does. All of time echoes at once, in that eternal moment and yet it is always now. When I was naked like that, stripped back to my skeleton, I was able to truly hear clearly for the first time. To paraphrase Dr. Martin Shaw: *myth is the story the land tells through us.*

The base notes to her song are geological to begin with. She wanted me to know and feel the seismic history of the land as I would know my beloved's sexual history. She wanted me to feel what moved this land so much that in her deep emotion she threw up mountains and tore down glaciers, melted down ice-caps with crying deep-lake tears. Unless you know stories of these important events how can you understand the upper layers to her?

The first people of the land I live upon had a story of how every layer of this island now called Tasmania which the first people call Trowenna or Latrowitta, was laid down by deities of sun and moon. I could feel how their story of the place surged up from the root-song of this place, but did not entirely contain or limit the song of the land itself. No one human culture was as much as this place was, no one species was ... Humans in general cannot sing a place, but are sung by the land, by the powers that live here, that much I felt, standing on Trowenna's mountain looking out toward her islands.

On the next higher octave, closer to the surface of sound, is the ancient dead, the fabulous beasts we name dinosaurs and mega fauna and the jet of ancient forests ... Here are to be found the songs that whistle through the bones of numerous animals that walk no more in the red realm, and finally the first Homo sapiens to ever walk here.

Alive humans tend to over extend our own importance, all of us for a start are vastly outnumbered by the dead. From the perspective of one who Sees, a genocide is never the end of a people. We bury the dead but we forget they are seeds ... A land's history is the history of its faerie races and spirit beings, some of which have stories intertwined with man and some that feel no connection with any human culture. Learning to belong to a land, I discovered over seven years of naturalizing, was less about becoming a member of a certain human social grouping and more about what Abrams would call Forgetting Human.

There were all these histories alive still in the eternal moment of the Place, there was the history of dreams, the history of things unspoken and forgotten. I was learning that a place has mouths and a digestive system that it eats and excretes. Consider the concept of the past, these histories I mention are not 'past' in any neat definitive way in the Otherworld. So whilst I am telling you that a place isn't limited to the life of man and the colonial atrocities and invasions and battles we visit upon each other on that land, memory is also a constant condition. There is no escaping it, we must pay heed to it, even if that's all we can ever do about it, we must never forget. We must find ways to love all that a place is in its inhuman beauty and horror. The human past is both less important, and in another way more important than we generally imagine.

The land is always chewing the cud of its echoes and regurgitating little gristly morsels. You can never hope to exorcise the past from a place, you can only come to learn where its mouths are and bear witness to the song of itself the place is trying to show you. All the ghosts, all the fae, all the echoes and monsters and angels and gods of a place are all part of this supreme expressiveness of the spirit of place, part of the wide-edged song of the land.

I began to learn from everything I encountered here with a humble mind, as uncluttered by preconceptions and the shrillness of modern discourse as I could manage. I discovered that pademelons and wallabies had their own dream of creation involving the world emerging from the marsupial pouch of some greater being. They were different in how they told and passed their stories, it was more like a shared dream of origin, mingled with the milky traces of their childhood. The fae beings of the wattle trees claimed to live along way off over the water until it was time for the flowering, and then they would come in a great procession, walking on a sky highway of levitating wattle down particles. Their stories seldom had much to do with people, until you met those who claimed to have dealt with the sorcerers of the old people.

Some of these spirits have adhered to the belief that sorcerers constitute a species apart from the rest of mankind and have no native race of any kind; others required me to prove I didn't think like a white fella. The main ways seemed not to arrogantly deny these non-human entities personhood or consider them all figments of an insubstantial imagination. Supremacy thinking of any kind, whether racial or species based was sure to cause failure. That and bringing too much mental chatter to their sacred site. 'We felt you coming a mile out with your busy white man head' a spirit once told me. 'You need to drop down into your belly more, or into your bones.'

Since then whenever I enter a place I know to be a site of power, I immediately stop talking in my head and drop my thoughts down into my belly. Then I let my ego and human identity come away as I walk, until in my heart's eye I am a skeleton moving through the bush. When I meet land spirits down to my bones like this I have usually been greeted in a non-hostile manner.

But before you can be in that state you will have to find a way to slough off pre-conceptions and shame associations about not belonging, to both be one with, and free of, history at the same time. If you struggle a lot with the guilt aspect of this may I suggest doing something tangible with it? Volunteer to help your local Aboriginal community in some manner or donate regular money to a First Nations health initiative, whatever you are most suited to. Shame does no one any good, not you and not the dispossessed or the murdered. There are tangible magical things you can do too, which we will cover in the Ancestral Burden chapter. But the important thing is to put the feeling into the work rather than nurture impotent guilt that causes paralysis. Because what is more useful at the end of the day? Active restorative justice or you to refrain from bonding with the land you were born on forever because you feel ancestral guilt?

The work we are going to do will still be necessary if, like my mother, you find yourself born upon your ancestral land. All of us have been alienated to some degree, even most indigenous people will have felt the impact of science trying to replace their creation mytho-realities, or rationalism mocking their spirit beliefs and worse still cultural (as well as actual) genocide where children were separated from parents and educated in missions. A breakage in the line of wisdom passage which sometimes resulted in story loss and thereby partial severance from participation in the dreaming life of their holy places.

1. A magical practitioner should understand the local spiritual topography. This will include all known stories about the creation of the place. A witch's covenstead extends to a three-mile radius from their hearth, so this is a good distance to define the Place you should focus on. The area you pay attention to may vary slightly from that broad rule, depending on the physical features of the land.

Within that area you will need to consider: where are the human dead buried? Both the recent dead and what, if anything, do we know about the ancient dead? Where are the places of most uninterrupted green life where forest life is least subject to human intrusion? Where do gateways to the Underworld open in the land to disgorge the dead and at what times do these gateways seem most active? Where might power re-emerge in the other direction from the Underworld in the form of fertile springs or wells or caves? Where are the highest peaks and where do the lines cross when you draw straight lines between them on a map? Is there anything of significance on these spots?

If you live in the UK and you're a practising occultist you are probably well aware of what ley lines or ghost roads you have passing through your immediate environment, but people like myself will have to start almost from scratch. It will be important to know as much about both the natural and human history of the spot as you can. Not only may this give you clues to where places of certain kinds of power may be, but it is just necessary for truly understanding a Place. The spirit of Place has a character, and like all of us their character is formed in part by experiences.

2. During this moon you are going to be doing a lot of walking out to sites you've learned about. When you do so, I would like you to practise walking meditation in that I don't want you to think about your human affairs but be mentally quiet and absorbed in observation of your environment. Notice the non-

human stories that are going on around you. Take rest in a spot that feels powerful and sit for a very long time without moving much. Observe how the place begins to continue to work around you as if you had become part of the forest. If you pay attention long enough you will begin to notice the subtle life of the place. I often say that the Sight should also be called the Noticing, because frequently the doings of spirit entities go on right before our eyes and we are too much in our own heads to see it.

3. When you begin to get a sense of where the holy places are and what spirits abide there you can take them offerings. It's best not to be too dogmatic about this because different spirit tribes will want different things. I've heard some people say 'why would the spirits here in Australia want cow's milk when cow's milk isn't native to the place?' Well, for a start, there are some faeries that seem to have migrated here along with the European plant life they are partially enmeshed with and they like milk.

Also, there is two hundred years' worth of milk drinkers dead in the soil. The same goes for things like rum, which some say is insulting to offer here because of the scourge that alcohol can be on indigenous health, but not every spirit has been human or had a close association with humans. So the rule of thumb is to follow what the individual asks for, just like you would if someone came to your house and you asked them if they wanted tea or coffee, you wouldn't say to them 'I'm sorry but I think coffee is problematic for people like you so I totally insist you become a tea drinker.' You would serve them coffee. This could be seen as a fine example of leading from one's magical convictions rather than socio-political ones.

4. Going back to your bones: Find a quiet power place out of doors where you are unlikely to be interrupted. Take with you a large cloak or blanket that you can wrap yourself up in like a shroud. Lie down upon the land whilst wrapped up in it and

begin to visualise yourself as a corpse. Over a period of days you watch from outside as the animals and birds of the place come and eat your flesh. Finally the ants and other insects come and swarm you back down to picked-clean bones. As you watch, contemplate that you will one day give your flesh to this land in this manner; this is a covenant between you and Place. When you have fed yourself to the Land in this manner, re-enter your bones. Move through your environment as a skeleton stripped of human markers and meet the spirits of the place in this form.

Repeat all of these steps for as long as the moon lasts. Take down notes of all your discoveries but don't fall into hubris by being too quick to think what you've discovered or been told is the be-all and end-all story of Place. There are as many subtle and not-so-subtle variations of those narratives as there are places and people to come together while they are sung or danced by the land.

Moon 7

The Bodies of the Witch

'What is the biggest difference do you think? Between your folk and people inside the hedge?' Lux asked.

Robin answered without hesitation. 'Their body makes a tight horizon around who they are. They identify with only one form, as if they are alone in the world.'

Lux frowned. 'What do you mean?'

'If outsiders look at me they would see a young man, poor, ditch-born, outlawed ... But that is not who's speaking to you really. I'm human, hob man, wolf, angel fire, my foremothers collectively, a child, an old man or many old men, mountains, Grandmother Land Herself, poetry, war, sadness at the state of war, eagles, flint, and honey ... They also are more than they know. Why identify only with the one small, body settlers want to chain us in? The church says we are immortal soul

> and yet they define the standing of one from the other based on sex and wealth. Why when one of my bodies is immortal would I chain myself to the parameters of one mortal form? It is ridiculous when the human form is just like a spearhead used to pierce our separation, to allow in the rushing of the true forms. For those who truly See, it all washes through and overlaps with this form in waves that are all as real and tangible as each other. To one such as I it is nonsense when people talk about ageing, scars or how pleasing the bone structure of someone as a measure of what beautiful is, for we do not see as mortals see. We faerie people see the fullness of the forms at all times, dancing in and out of focus.'
> (Robin Goodfellow in the *Lux De Rue Novels*)

We all know the witch embodies revolution, or to some the threat of revolution. The body of the witch is, after all, a body that has been stripped, examined, pricked, poked, tortured and marginalized as grotesquery. The final insult was to be no longer feared, made into a joke, an embarrassing memory of the magical thinking of Europe's ancestors. Afterwards, when she had been forgotten, many of the more edgy tropes of rebellion migrated into the arts. In the Romantic Age it was understood that the figure of the poet was now the one who embodied revolution. Peter Grey rightly notes the migratory roots of this concept, from the witch, to the poet, and from the poet back through to the self-consciously revolutionary practitioner of witchcraft in modern times.

But what does it mean to embody revolution? What does it mean to be the owner of the body that exists amid the flux of revolution? If one is a manifestation of the powers outside the hedge and one forms a community of Others, does that periphery now become a new centre? Doesn't the radical become a new dogma? Or is a dynamic tension possible, a third state, a dance we might equate with the strong presence of life force?

Somewhere in the consideration of these questions we come to the mindset necessary to truly see the witch's body in the fullness of its forms.

We can learn a lot from the mythic figure of the witch, even if we don't identify as one ourselves. It can teach us about how not to get caught up in the game of opposites. While you are still defining yourself in opposition to the establishment you are still reacting to them, they are still in control of you. To embody revolution is something different again. It is to be not just a body that can't be adequately categorized or defended in any civil rights movement, or even to require others to recognise a single ambiguity with terminology; it is, in fact, to be *bodies*.

To embody revolution is to become so free from the paradigm that next to everyone else is caught up in that original thoughts are possible, chaotic new possibilities arise, magic is potentialised. If you came here to learn how to rock the cradle of Fate, which Robert Cochrane told us 'nurses the infant soul' then we are going to have to be capable of being aware of the rocking. Every act of sorcery is a revolution; it is an anomaly, a breaking of the general rule. The devil, the Lucifer, has become for many the ultimate embodiment of revolution. He is the Other, so you can never create orthodoxy around him or around witches, without losing sight of Him. For he is by nature always in motion, like Eliphas Levi's comet was to the fixed star.

The body has been made political territory since humans first decided to impose their creeds on how we were allowed to use our own bodies. A witch must always be in a state of transformation and synthesis of opposites, rather than reactions against them and cunning tricks are best deployed when fighting leviathans. I have one trick I call 'Don't Look the Medusa Directly in the Face'. Mirrors are smarter ways to get a look at her.

Let me provide an example. For a very long time now society has tried to impose a certain kind of feminine ideal on women, I think this is inarguable regardless of how you are aligned politically. That's not to say that 'the patriarchy', (or whatever you like to call the ideology imposing it) is made up of all-male members mind you … Now let's say some women and supporters recognise this and react against it, instead utterly refusing any of the trappings of femininity without thought, even if they actually like them, because the answer is to be the opposite to everything you've been told to be. What we end up with here is a movement still controlled by the patriarchy as prime mover, it made a move, you flipped it and reversed its decree and lived by that inverse decree even if it meant giving up things you didn't want to be seen to enjoy.

Here this movement would have 'looked the Medusa in the face' and like the Medusa's heart, it would turn to immoveable stone. What if instead we find cunning ways to work around the Medusa and nullify her power without entering into her narrative? Because once you enter the terms of a dispute with another power you do so within the confines of certain fateful outcomes. But if you are the one to determine the terms of the engagements there may be ways to become the hand that rocks the cradle.

So far the people have attempted to recover from the above-mentioned problem in a few different ways. One was throw the beauty baby out with the bathwater entirely by refusing to engage with their appearance aesthetically. Another is to broadly claim 'all women are beautiful', a third option responds to that by questioning why women must be beautiful at all in order to have high self-esteem.

All of these reactions are perfectly valid, yet none of them fully undercuts the premise the whole thing is based on in the first place: which is that we have only one form, and that its appearance alone is able to express our nature or convictions in some way. But the thing with witches (and I apologies to all occultists and those planned on undertaking a different magical tradition, but witchcraft has a lot to teach us in this instance) is that they never had just one body, or a single form.

Sorcerers of old were understood to have other bodies, a hidden shadow they could send to hag someone, or various animal forms that could be projected from their human body. Some of them were really wolves, or a black dog that could free itself to go hunting the souls of those fated to die. Witches in particular were considered to use 'glamours' to accomplish this, and of course it would have to be that way, because anything that was different to the one true body must be situated as an illusion within the God and the Devil, Truth and Illusion paradigm.

More recently in history the talented artist and occultist Austin Osman Spare provides us with a salient example of the many bodies of the witch. One of the formative influences upon the young Spare was an older woman often referred to as Witch Patterson. Spare told of how she could change her appearance from her mature form to that of a much younger woman, probably her own younger self, and could bring future events to visible manifestation for those who queried her on divination. In other words she could bring someone with her into the condition of the Witch's Sabbath, (that space that exists at once in all times, places and conditions) and allow the invisible to become visible. She was able to move around in the 'fullness of her forms' and to take a receptive party there with her. Even her portrait refused to have only one face and was said to morph between forms. In other words, she was a witch.

When I speak of the witch embodying revolution, most will think I mean the statement politically, but it does not always have to be taken in that way, even though the implications of the witch's many bodies is indeed potentially politically revolutionary. If we knew how to work on our other forms we'd not place so much weight upon the one. If, like Mrs. Patterson, we had the power to show our other forms to each other we would spend less money trying to prevent ageing. All of these things are potentially revolutionary, but this is only part of the point. The world of man is only ever part of the point.

The bodies of the witch are in a state of revolution at all times because they fluctuate in power, with certain skins gaining more power at certain times of the lunar and solar cycles as we pass through one of the ways time is experienced. The forms are never fully still, they move and reform like liquid, and like the tide of the ocean they are pulled and affected by the moon. This is one of the reasons that the influence of the moon is so important in magic.

Waxing Moon

A lot of people assume magic comes from somewhere outside the body, in defiance of the body and the natural order of things, a supernatural force. But if there's an idea we could most do well to be rid of it is this one. There is a deep intelligence in this body we walk around in; it forms the focal point of numerous bodies of knowledge which are older than it. I refer to the most immediate of these bodies as the Double or the fetch.

You might think you are unaware of having more than one body but as the fetch is integral with your physical body you have been, in fact, feeling it your entire life without knowing what it was. Most likely you haven't been encouraged to pay attention. You may have been actively told not to pay attention to your body, not to fidget in class or wander where your flesh led you. Nevertheless you have felt its presence in things which we call 'gut feelings'. Some European cultures taught that a person's Double was housed in a particular organ, such as the liver or heart. So you might say that to our forebears, we were a body containing organs that were houses for other bodies that could emerge independently. The fetch can be projected from the body through the mouth or other liminal place on the body into other skins, usually animals. A fetch is simply an activated Double, or a sorcerously potent Double.

Not only does our upbringing discourage the fetch, a lot of

popular spiritual practices have us meditating and concentrating on things we see in our heads. Working with the fetch is not like that and so some people find it hard to take the work seriously as a spiritual endeavour for this reason, but those who are capable of seeing differently obtain great power through this simple sounding work. Most importantly they become aware of the use of more than one body, which takes an enormous pressure off our daytime body! Eating disorders are a prime example of a body over-loaded with pressure to express itself by controlling the shape of the only body society gives value to, the one body which is expected to support and express an entire identity's worth of meaning.

The key to fetch work is to slow down and focus on the details of each practice as though the whole of the Work were to be found in that one simple act of attention. Each practice here has hidden layers of profundity for those who are truly paying attention. Always remember, the devil is in the details!

One old way of knowing the presence of the fetch in the body is through the body's involuntary motions and impulses. The way to strengthen the fetch is through beginning to offer it some freedom, attention and respect. After all, this is the part of ourselves that has been most damaged and demonized by the age we live in, both by mainstream religion and its hatred for the animal within, by materialism, by advertising and by the taming shackles of modern capitalism. Of all the work our tradition does in training witches, it is this work that is the most arduous and the most resisted whilst seemingly the most simple.

As the source of involuntary movements was unknown scientifically in the past, naturally our ancestors saw these things as coming from the Unseen. Today many struggle to get back to their fetch's voice because these things have been 'explained away' by science. But merely knowing how the brain registers fetch activity does not explain away the existence of the fetch. Nervous system activity is just a different language for the same thing, a helpful terminology for dealing with matters of health and medical emergencies, but a language lacking in a few empowering facets of magical language.

When it comes to scientific materialism and the Craft, it might be said that you can only serve one master and a meeting with your fetch will require the sacrifice of your Western ego. Especially its belief that it owns the one meta-narrative to explain all things for all time. Consider our shared Western hubris a sacrifice you will make at the door of the Pale People before you enter the door in the hill. A sacrifice you will have to continue making for the rest of your life whenever you are forced to choose between your soul's answer and the answer given to you by society. Eventually you will find ways to hold both at the same time, with each emerging in the arena where it's most useful. No explanation for why we have involuntary motion can change the fact that it is precisely in that unconscious part of the mind that the fetch emerges from and fills out the skins we ride in during the witch's night-flight. If these questions come up for you or block you, make note of them in your journal under a section in the back that you should mark as Rinse and Repeat. We will return to this data during the thirteenth moon.

It is interesting, particularly for those of us located in Tasmania to note that there are records that the Tasmanian Aboriginals shared the same belief that unexplained trembling or palpitations of the heart could be used as a form of divination. In George Augustus Robinson's *Friendly Mission* he mentions on more than one occasion how one of the Aboriginal men, usually a man of high standing, would alert the others to the fact that he was trembling for no reason or that his heart was beating very hard. The others of his clan would become nervous because this was the man's 'devil' who lived in his chest alerting them to danger. The other body was strong enough in these men that the pumping or trembling could be easily observed by bystanders.

For the above reasons, when working with the fetch we should adopt forms of divination that rely on the body's involuntary movements, such as pendulum, dowsing rod and collection casting. But it should be remembered that even the seemingly random choice method of selecting tarot cards is a way of letting the mute fetch speak to you through images and archetypes.

Involuntary Motions and Traditional Associations

Here is a list of traditional beliefs about involuntary body signals drawn from folklore known to me. Please keep in mind they are meant to be *unexplained*. If you have a condition like hay fever and your nose itches for instance it is probably less significant. Usually once you start paying attention to these signs you will find yourself sensing the significance of certain bodily feelings over certain others. You will also discover that these traditional meanings are only a jump-off point. Your fetch will probably develop a unique language to communicate with you, and the hairs on the back of your neck rising might mean something entirely different to you than to someone else.

The more you listen the more your fetch will speak to you and the louder the 'quiet voice inside the stomach and blood' will seem. Note down what you discover in your magical journal, recording any resistance you feel in the back under 'Rinse and Repeat'.

Nose Itches: Your fetch is letting you know that someone is thinking about you, possibly news is coming to you.

Ear Rings: Your fetch is warning you that people are talking about you.

Itchy Ears: People are talking about you again, right for spite, left for love. If it's spite, put some spit on your finger and touch your earlobe with it, this is believed to make the person speaking ill of you bite their tongue!

Palm Itches: Money coming, if it's the right hand don't scratch it. If it's your left it's money going out so scratch it away.

Right Eye Itches or Twitches: Traditionally this was your fetch telling you that something is going to happen, something lucky, like seeing your lover.

Tripping or Stumbling: Your fetch is active in your body and preparing to fly or do battle.

Shivers: Someone is walking on your future grave or someone has just passed over nearby.

Yawning: Your Fetch is already wandering away from your body while you are still awake, cover your mouth with your hand to prevent entrance of an evil spirit while you're vulnerable.

Accidental tongue biting: You've recently said something your fetch knows to be false.

Tingling Lips: Signals the presence of the fetch mate trying to touch you or kiss you.

Sneeze: Fetch leaves the body momentarily during a sneeze. And yet the ability to do so and still re-enter signals that one is truly one of the living, so a baby's first sneeze is significant. Sneeze 'once for a wish, twice for a kiss, three for a letter, four for something better'.

Coughing: Sudden entrance of a devil (spirit, powerful spirit) into the person who wishes to communicate or be acknowledged in some way. An unexplained coughing fit may be a request for the witch to enter oracular trance. Coughing that leads to unexplained retching is a stronger version of this.

Itchy Feet: A journey or some kind of movement is required.

Itch on the crown of the head: Advancement in the world is predicted.

Pricking in the Thumbs: Something wicked this way comes!

Unexplained sudden ill temper: A querulous, predatory fetch that needs to leave the body on a mission or there are angry dead nearby who need to be cleared.

Trembling: Continuous trembling linked to no known health or temperature reason, as opposed to a light shiver, is a very strong message from the fetch. Could mean imminent danger, pull your car over, stop what you are doing; change the course of where you are walking.

Heart Beating Fast: The presence of the Other, a strong spirit.

Hair Raising: The hair rising up on the back of the neck or arms is associated with the Other but more usually of the fae or the dead – though this breakdown doesn't hold true for everyone.

Unexplained Tears: Another common response to strong fae presence or that of a god.

Paralysis: Full body paralysis (once cleared of health problems) or pressure on the chest is a sign of being hagged, often by another practitioner or their helper spirit.

Nose Bleed: A great deal of power is moving through your the body, especially fire in the head, this is the fetch's way of taking the pressure. Cutting a witch 'above the breath' was used in the past to temporarily neutralize another practitioner's power.

Sexual Arousal: Sudden unexplained sexual arousal is an indicator of the presence of a spirit of strong power or sexual nature, or some other catalyst moving power around in great quantities. Illicit magic being worked on you is often given away in this manner.

Need to Urinate: Sudden needs to urinate are connected with a nervous response. This means your fetch is agitated and if you see no rational reason to be then you will want to find out why. Sometimes it knows things you aren't conscious of knowing about your environment and the people.

Need to Void Bowels: Especially if sudden and happening after magic with no health related issue known, this can indicate the fetch is removing a power obstruction or for some people, that they are walking over ground with a strong Underworldly pull.

Mouth Watering: If you are not hungry yourself and didn't just see food yet your mouth still waters, the fetch is hungry and requires nourishment.

Untimely Menstruation: A woman who suddenly bleeds when it is not her time and for whom this doesn't usually happen may have received power or a message from the Foremothers.

Practical Tips: Observation of involuntary bodily motions

Begin to take note of your involuntary bodily signals based on traditional lore. Write down anything you notice in your magical journal, especially anything that relates to signs from your fetch that might be unique ways of sending messages that do not appear in the list. It may sound strange or silly to be paying this much attention to every sneeze and itch, but just think of the heightened bodily awareness you are developing! Think of how much more 'in their body' our ancestors must have been for focusing on their bodily sensations in this manner. Today we engage our brain and eyes in most work and even our recreation but we spend little time listening to the body, when the innate knowing of the body is our most important piece of divinatory equipment.

Full Moon: Fullness of Forms

After working on the above during the waxing moon you will be ready to do the following for the three nights where the moon is fullest.

Lie down and get comfortable. Work through bringing each of your senses to conscious awareness. At first you will begin with one at a time, this means you should leave your eyes open during 'sight' but close them during 'sound'. Pay as much attention as you can to every bit of sensory input that you might have been ignoring. Try not to judge it as good or bad stimuli, just observe it, much in the manner of any Buddhist mindfulness training.

Now begin to layer the attention to the senses one over the other, consciously 'forgetting' the words for each sense, settling into a single united sensory awareness that just 'receives' without distinction between sound, sight, touch, taste and smell.

Forget that you ever knew words, forget that you can even speak and try to experience the world around you as though you have never seen the objects around you before. Focus on this until an almost eerie newness and sense of alien-ness is cast over the things you are looking at.

Now I want you to turn your attention inward to that one sense that is all the senses: your essential awareness. Behind that sense is an all-over tingling sensation or a buzzing or pulsating, this is your essential Awareness of Being that existed before you were born and will continue after you die.

Feel yourself being breathed into being in every moment by this immense Darkness that underpins your essential awareness, your body and everything else that you are; the darkness of that which is within or below the surface where the hidden forms lie.

Draw your focused but relaxed attention over the area where your awareness of being extends to. Begin to breathe a little faster to agitate and shake things up. Begin to rock or sway or shudder slightly, this motion may come naturally to you but if it doesn't make this slight movement on purpose. Feel the light motion shaking the fabric of your other forms. Notice what you feel. Do you experience any body dysmorphia? Any sense of having wings or claws or being another shape? Slowly start to transfer this shaking and seething to your subtle bodies so that your daytime body becomes still but still feels like you are trembling all over. Mentally ask your bodies to reveal all of their forms and shapes. Drop these words down into the darkness behind creation, starting in your head, letting the message overflow into your ribs and finally into your hips.

Animal forms reveal yourselves

The primal atavisms of the fetch in its beast forms are called to seethe to the surface first. Trembling and breathe it free just enough that you can feel it viscerally, feel its feathery/furry/scaly body pulling free or even just rising to the surface to infiltrate your human skin with hair or feathers growing through the skin. Allow it to settle back down into the guts or heart. Notice where it settles. Does it lodge in a particular organ?

Exhalation of the Blood reveal yourself

The Double of a person is called on here, the second more subtle body that is the exhalation of the living blood, or the blood soul, one of the parts that sometimes goes forth in flight. Feel it tugging apart from sticky closeness with your daytime body, until you are aware of its shimmering motion being separate from the heavier of the two forms. Slowly allow the Double to settle back down into the blood.

Soul of the Bones show yourself

This is the deepest coming forth. See in vision your daytime skin being peeled back and turning inside out to reveal the bones on the outside and the flesh on the inside. This back to front self reveals that the Holy Daimon, your immortal form, is truly both all around you and at the core of you at the same time, the central reality from which you manifest outward into form. See this glowing skeleton begin to draw in the light that surrounds you as aura and join both light body and skeleton until you feel the presence of the Soul of the Bones. Exhale and allow yourself to re-ravel and the daimon to settle into its paradox state of central bones and surrounding holy-spirit.

Other-Skin, Blood and Bone bodies show yourselves

Now allow time for any other bodies that make up your being to rise to the surface. Some of them may make requests to be acknowledged or better incorporated in some way, or even perhaps merged with another form. They may consist of extra animal skins that were gifted by ancestors who once wore those skins, or (like me) you may possess forms of more than one sex, or other orders of non-human creature. You should try not to decide you have any idea what will come until you try it. And each time you try you should encounter yourself with the same open attitude.

When you feel ready, settle everything into place and take some deep grounding breaths.

When you repeat this technique you can omit the structure if you wish and just allow each of the Skins to reveal themselves, express anything they might need or want for their well-being and subside back into your Whole. If a new form has been gifted to the sorcerer in a dream or other spirit-walk then it should be acknowledge and integrated during such a session.

If during the daily repetition nothing comes forward at all and everything remains in stillness, simply move your awareness over the other parts you know to be there, acknowledging them, naming them and finishing.

Waning Moon

Each night of the waning moon should be designated to a different one of the forms that you have discovered during the full moon. Focus on that form until you can feel it in great detail, greet it and extend your awareness into it. When it feels right to do so, attempt to move it around beyond the physical parameters of your daytime body. This may feel like stretching wings or extra limbs, try it in different directions without moving your human form off the bed. You may not work long on this before you feel the shape burst forth from your chest and are running or flying in it. Alternatively, this other shape may want to move around together with your daylight body, in which case you should allow yourself to be led by the fetch into whatever types of motion it prefers. You may find you drop down on all fours or engage in a kind of swaying trance-dance.

Each night of the waning moon, repeat this process with a

different form. If you have only found one extra one you will simply need to repeat the full moon exercise on the night in-between to give anything else a chance to rise to the surface.

Don't be surprised to encounter other forms that are simply yourself at different life phases. Remember, time doesn't work the same in the Otherworld, so a child-you and an old person-you exist in there also.

Dark Moon

During the three days where the moon is darkest we shall experiment with how your forms are 'fed'. For some fetches who like to appear as beasts this is a literal kind of eating, involving running or flight which ends in the consumption of some kind of spirit prey. But this is not true for all forms; some require other forms of nourishment. Now is the time to find out what they are. One of the subtler things that some forms require is attention. Here the old adage, heeding is feeding, becomes important.

Find a way if you can to represent that shape in some way that potentially allows it to be comprehended by other humans. This could take the shape of a mummified bird in the case of one of my forms, or an artwork. Either way, you need to find something that either looks like or symbolically represents this other form. Anoint the object with a drop of your own blood and express verbally: this is one of my forms.

You may like to add some words to convey that it is as real as your physical body. Even if this is something you are not yet able to feel, affirming it has power. Because it is an affirmation of the state we are hoping to move towards here. When you are able to become aware as truly being these other things as much as you are human in this body, you will become so much harder to manipulate.

Over time you will cease to be impressed by beauty that exists only in one of the bodies if it isn't equally represented in the others. You will cease to feel as if ageing is real, because you will become familiar both with the part of you that can never be old and the part of you that has always been old. A sorcerer who is alive in the continuous revolution of her own bodies can never be killed. Even if he is crippled he cannot be contained to a chair. Angst over the fact her face and figure do not entirely convey the substance of her character will cease to seem so important. The company of others who are chosen for perceiving his other forms and how attracted he is to theirs, as well as the daylight body, will cease to be important. In short, the witch is set free, not of the body, but of the *singularity* of the image.

Moon 8

Addressing the Ancestral Burden

Part of the work of the necromancer is to act in many ways as a spiritual midwife between the worlds both spiritual and physical and to dust off the detritus that often clings to the soul in the present world and the worlds beyond. Unfortunately, as we live in the evils of empire, many souls are not given the proper rites and, like the blood of Abel, cry up constantly from the earth seeking vengeance. This is not a new problem by any stretch of the imagination, however, I can't help but to think that what we are seeing in our culture is the result of centuries of bloodshed with the dead, righteous and unrighteous, playing out a war in which the living are now unconscious participants.

Improperly cared for in death, souls can become every bit as feral as fierce alley cats and strike out at the living in

> their confused states. It is for this reason that many cultures preserve some form of placation for the ferocious dead, those who died in an unwashed state or those who in life experienced trauma. The blood soaked history of the United States with a long history of exploitation, slavery, war, and violence against the impoverished has created a mass grave where the wrathful dead walk side-by-side with the living and 'suck the purest of your blood and open wounds which are almost always mortal' (Kardec). The psycho-spiritual wounds of the living become entry points for the dead to influence the living, often coercing them to play out the traumas they themselves experienced.
> (Michael Sebastion Lux)

We are our ancestors walking.

What we are walking on is the dead.

The foundations of our world are on and have been built by the dead.

We try to avoid these key facts with taboos about walking over graves and generally keeping cemeteries away from food growing areas, so we don't directly contemplate the connection – the way our world is built on the back of theirs, of their labour, of their nitrogen … Whilst we've tried numerous ways to exorcise their visible presence from our immediate environment the dead persist in numbers too numerous to be noticeable, a blip of the numinous, too common for the human senses to any longer register the signals. The dead are like a smell so pervasive we can no longer smell it.

We who call ourselves the living are in fact interactive sites of what Austin Osman Spare called atavistic resurgences; this is to say that all the creatures and other humans that went into making us up live on as echoes in our deep being, surging to surface at certain times. It is from these resurgences that the witch comes to know the multiple bodies, making us a many-headed being with fully functioning bodies that exist in different simultaneous realities. We possess more heads than we can take selfies of, and no one will ever give us a 'like' for them on Facebook.

In terms of our mental health, it is that which we are unconscious of that is in control. We are swimming around in a soup of influences that do not have their origin in our declared will. So when teachers, like my first witchcraft mentor, tell you it's all about will and the control over yourself to give up addictions and sort yourself out by your bootstraps, the matter might not always be so simple. Of course, if it were it would be easier and less people would be struggling with their mental health and addictions. What if the problem doesn't lie inside the individual? Or even their victimization history? It's simpler certainly to blame the individual for insufficient will but it's messier, and more complex to consider what is at the root of the drive they feel and from whence it came.

Ancestral curses might sound like the stuff of fairytales. They are, and this is why they are one of the most important hidden-in-plain-sight facts about life. Pretty much everyone has inherited not only characteristics but family ghosts. Those ancestral dead who remain attached to the red thread of the family line which causes individuals to generally be the source of hauntings rather than buildings. At times of emergency they lend us their skills, advice and strengths yet these beings are not necessarily any more perfected than you and I. Like all humans they occupy every rung on the ladder from very wise to very ignorant and from good to evil with all the grades of trickster in between. It would be very foolish indeed to entirely cede one's judgement to 'the ancestors', with some naïve belief they've been perfected in both motives and vision by death. When ancestor-venerating people talk about 'ancestors' they seem to mean specific dead people who are remembered by name for some reason of some power, skill, miracles, or who tangibly help the community in smaller ongoing ways.

Ancestors can possess distinct biases towards certain behaviour over others, such as being pro-reproduction, even when your circumstances don't really favour the idea. This is part of the reason why your 'ancestors' shouldn't just consist of your dead blood-kin but of representatives of groups that have gone up to making your life in general. Who among the dead do you have to thank for the life you live today and how can you honour them also?

Because the Eternal Sabbat exists in a space where all times are one time, sorcerers have a tendency to talk about history as though they were there for it! In a way we were. The wider historical picture of Place often seems like the backdrop of our story because the line between healing the individual's relations with the fabric of life and *becoming* the fabric of life can be very hazy indeed. This may make it hard to know exactly what or who among the dead require our attention.

We will learn though, as we go along that our ancestral work will be more often about healing and expiating the sins (meaning in this context whatever the spirit perceives as a heaviness upon them, and usually that heaviness is shame rather than the perceived crime itself) that lie upon our own forebears as it is about gaining wondrous knowledge from wise dead folk. Eventually if we work diligently the truly powerful and wise individuals in our up-line will reveal themselves. Magic works don't tend to spring out of nowhere and somewhere in your forebears there was someone like you.

The first step in being able to properly relate to the dead is to stop identifying solely with your daylight body's identity when you have been present throughout history and lived as many things. After having left your bundle and reduced yourself to your bones you are essentially in the state of the dead who die well. To properly do away with limiting notions that hold us back from the performance of more powerful sorcery requires us to become like one of the great dead who made the transition in the most profound state of consciousness and surrendered their limitations, to see with hollow eyes of blinding sight the true pettiness of our mortal grasping to any singular identity. We can choose to relinquish that now, or the many deaths that follow the in-gathering we call physical death will pull it from our hands one day anyway. I for one would rather do this work on my own terms.

For if there's one thing the wise dead see clearly on, it's that. They care less about what people think of them, they often regret having lived for other people's notions of them. With the less wise death their advice on your life may be skewed by their own traumas or their own failings, which they may try to make up for through you, attempting to turn your life into their do-over. You are likely to be unaware because these drives to live out certain stories will arise from the unconscious level and someone else who knows you well is more likely to be able to see them than you. In this way certain pre-occupations and problems can play out through generation after generation. Despite these failings, their vision of their own life is usually panoramic and placed in context by the scope of eternity.

When we die our daylight body will rot and become part of one land, one sky, one water system. The dead know this and the better sort among them take heed of it, it starts to matter less whether in life they were designated male or female, black or white, rich or poor. The wise dead understand we all take up the same space in the ground regardless of the tomb above it. Only those who are stuck in their ego and unwilling to fully experience the mystery of the Unworld seem to continue to grab at their old assumptions until they are finally voided into an unheeding abyss which recycles much of what they are made from. The story occult observation tells you about the processes of birth, life, death and what lies after are not the stuff of comforting tales for the masses, they match more with what you know already about Nature and her red claws and teeth. But, of course, Nature makes rainbows and flowers as well and there is much of comfort to be known for those who don't expect easy answers.

The dead have access to a new authenticity outside of social labels and constraints, so they sometimes see where they gave themselves away to please others and hid vital parts of themselves. For this reason the most frequent request from the dead is your awareness of them and their true story. Not the one they sanitized even in their journal and correspondence, but the real one. This isn't about the opinions of the living so much as it is about releasing an unspent energy which is preventing them completing their death process. To die with unspoken words or unfinished deeds creates an echo, a sort of unresolved wave of power that must be grounded into our world in some way. With ancestral dead this will often mean discovering uncomfortable truths about the people you descend from. They may need to confess to you a story where they did something terrible.

Like everything we've covered so far we should avoid a shame response at all costs. Whatever your ancestors did has been there, hanging over you like a dark cloud you weren't aware of until now, this is the good moment, the uncomfortable moment of healing, where the heaviness is finally being brought to light. Curses that continue 'to the seventh generation' and such might sound unfair, and really, they are, but so are a lot of things about how inheritance works. Nobody says it's not fair when they realise they inherited short-sightedness from their parents, and it's a bit like that with the crimes of the fathers. It isn't fair, you didn't do it, yet nonetheless its been hanging over your life in some way since you were born and you are only now able to see it and thus exorcise it.

There can be a great deal of healing just in owning something. In saying: 'yes I not only spring from those that did these things but until now my behaviour has perpetuated it. From this moment on the curse is broken.' You can start doing this sort of thing just via family research. Most people shy away from the stories of the bad ancestors, preferring to focus on the achievements of the side of the family they are proud of. And whilst I understand this impulse all too deeply, I must insist that you pay attention to all possible branches of your family tree so you can root out whatever lurks in the shadows.

Then you will want to find out about your non-blood ancestors, those whose work or influence your life owes something to. You will of course have far too many options to choose from, so use your intuition as to where you're guided on this front. Find out as much as you can and when you have a few forebears, both bloodline ancestors and others, begin to collect things that relate to them. It might be relics of theirs, things they owned when they were alive, copies of their photograph or portrait, pictures of things that would have meant something deep and lasting to them. To measure whether you've done enough research on a person or not you need simply ask yourself if you can identify what these would be?

Once you have about five or six dead people you feel intuitively drawn to you will begin to make preparations for hosting a dumb supper for these spirits. Before we can get very far with such a plan we need to talk about methods of communication between yourself and the dead. Some of you will already be aware that you possess what we call Second Sight, others of you do but don't realise it yet and others still will need to work on developing this faculty. The best way to approach this is via the 'don't look the Medusa in the face' principle I mentioned earlier. Treat something as a problem that needs to be worked on, focus on it and own it as your problem, or your weakness and it is likely to become a real stumbling block for you.

Instead go around the obstacle and don't think too much about it. Get yourself a pendulum, and/or a spirit board and a black shew stone or black scrying mirror. Give the spirits a lot of tools and props through which to communicate with you. This way whilst you are busy listening to your fetch and your pendulum the voices and the other forms of non verbal communication are likely to open up in the space this activity leaves in your routine this month. Before you begin using your pendulum to practise communicating with them, I want you to sit in silence for at least five minutes. Not only do I not want you to speak or move very much but your mental attitude should be on the side of quiet and receptivity.

If you have begun to acquire objects for the dead as mentioned above, put them on some sort of shrine space. This will provide a good focal point for your work. Sit in stillness before the shrine and allow at least five minutes of stillness before asking questions with your pendulum or other divinatory method. Some spirits begin to develop unique systems with practitioners who are not terribly Sighted in the traditional sense of hearing and seeing the dead, such as collection casting based on their relics, where objects that used to belong to them mean certain answers known only to the two of them. These kind of unique styles of divining the intentions and thoughts of the dead are just as valid as possessing natural Second Sight, as long as they get the job done. Usually once you've stopped focusing on whether you can see or hear them you start to hear and see them!

The importance of a Dumb Supper is that it's a bordered occasion you can send out an invitation to and see who arrives. This can be important because sometimes the ancestors who choose to step forward to work with you are not the ones who you thought they would be; you may not have even collected any relics or images of them.

The Dumb Supper:

It would be fortunate if you started your thirteen-moon journey at a time where this moon falls around the Hallows, though this is not at all necessary. If this is not possible merely selecting the dark of the moon will answer to the task. Although one might notice slightly more tendency for spirits to manifest to visible sight during the full of the moon, the dead are known to hunger most around the nights where no moonlight bathes the earth with the rays of the heavens.

Plan the supper in advance and send out invitations, just as you would to any party of people. The only difference will be that instead of posting them, you will be burning them to send them into the unseen. When the hour of their scheduled arrival comes you will have set a table in a darkened room. This will contain either a place for each intended guest, or in the case of space constraints, a communal setting for the dead. When you go to the door to let them inside you will not speak aloud and you should walk backwards wherever possible.

Take a seat in conditions that are as close to dark as allows you to still perceive the food and knives and forks, but only faintly. What you have cooked for the night may be influenced by your family traditions. Some traditions that practise necromancy believe that salt is baneful to the dead, whereas others believe it is attractive to the point of distracting. In such cases I think it's best to follow whatever conforms with your pre-existing culture or belief system, or if there is one your dead relatives subscribed to. The nine vegetable mash used for All Hallows dumb supper in my tradition includes salt as one of its prescribed ingredients. Whatever you decide in regards to salt, you will need to cook something hot as the dead seemingly universally appreciate heat.

When you take a seat begin to eat your food in silence, not looking directly at the other places at the table. While you eat, meditate on how your ancestors live inside you, connected with your guts, your hips, your blood, living on inside you. Mentally invite them to consume the virtues of the meal. You may find if you are the natural medium sort that you have experiences of actually being each of the dead. Otherwise you may perceive them as present across the table from you. As you perceive their definite arrival and note their identity pour them water and acknowledge them by passing it across in their direction or drinking in on their behalf if you are filled with a sudden and unnatural thirst.

This practice is referred to as 'drenching the ghosts'. Visualise the water pouring right through you down into the Underworld, filling the mouths of the thirsty dead. While the meal is in progress pay close attention to all of your sense for sources of information, as the dead won't always communicate in words. Part of how the communion precedes will depend on the visitors, and the other upon your own capacities when it comes to communication methods. You may find yourself feeling things, as if your hands had become arthritic and gnarled, or seeing images in your mind of memories that are not your own. Or you may simply hear voices competing to be heard. Try to acknowledge one in your mind and turn your attention to them, indicating that others will be heard in an order.

One of the things I've learned from interacting with the spirits of dead relatives is that older family members are not the person you knew as a child, or even as an adult. The part of one's self we might show to our grandchildren or children is a very different side to the way the person sees themselves as a whole adult, or how a lover sees them. A great deal is sanitized or just not shared in most familial settings. Communicating with the dead is different. There is less of a filter and so you are probably going to find out some things about Grannie that you didn't know about her during life. One of the most profound things you might come to know is what it *feels* like to be her. To like or dislike the same foods she did and to see memories through her eyes. These kinds of experiences can have revolutionary impacts on your life and how you see others.

When the meal comes to its natural termination, drink to the health of your dead and quietly show them out the way they came. In your heart tell them you will see them again soon. By the time you have finished this rite you should have a good idea which of your ancestors (whether they be blood, spirit or location ancestors) will be most suitable for ongoing work. Whilst a lot of power will rest with the ones less 'suitable', it is always best to learn a technique with an easy case first rather than a hard one.

You'll be able to tell which are most appropriate because they will be the ones who most dominated the 'conversation' during the Dumb Supper, the ones you made the deepest connection with that left the strongest impression on you. For those people, you will want to acquire some kind of spirit vessel, which will serve as a reliquary and feeding station for the spirit. It may be an actual urn designed for human ashes, into which you will place the person's grave dirt, ashes or relics. Depending on how the deceased individual feels about their prior existence they may or may not want to be remembered with a photograph, and they may have preferences about whether to be shown as you remember them or whilst at the age they regard as their prime.

You should pour fresh water for your dead between once a day and once a week, depending on how seriously you are working with them. The harder you work your spirits the greater their needs will be. Most of them will refrain from doing any big work to keep what is left of their vital force and won't expend any of it in the work you require until you have proved their upkeep will be maintained. During this time period you can begin to prepare them for the work required by opening them to new possibilities. Show them things they might not yet be aware of, such as the fact they can move to any location on the planet just from mentally setting an intention to be at that place.

Whilst this may seem an obvious skill once disembodied, it is rare for the dead to discover it on their own unless they are the shade of some spiritually developed individual or occultist. Most only walk the same familiar paths they took in life.

Once a dead person realises they are no longer bound by some of the old limitations this can be used to create a snowball effect where limitation after limitation starts coming down. There is one thing in particular that you want them to be able to let go of and that is the burden of their sins, as we discussed earlier – the weight that is primarily shame.

As people age many become increasingly calcified in their view of things and refuse to remain supple or to develop with the age they are witnessing. Those who die in that condition usually remain unyielding and stuck in certain repetitive loops of behaviour and feeling. These can constitute a person's own private hell. A hell-loop that keeps playing itself out, the complexity or simplicity of the knot they are in will generally determine whether their afterlife seems more like a purgatory or a hell.

The difference between the purgatory and hell when observed through the eyes of someone experimental in their attitude to the otherworld, rather than doctrinal, is that no higher authority inflicts their suffering. They can leave that state they are in through a simple change of perspective. Whilst it's simple once someone finds the knack in the absence of a Sin Eater it is something that the spirit must do for themselves. You can only show them how free they are now in a number of other ways to increase their confidence to the point where they realise they are *truly* free of every doctrine that bound them in life, every prejudice, even their own actions are the doings of a dead person they don't have to be anymore. They have the chance for the ultimate do-over, and without a body carrying flesh-memories and trauma this can be remarkably simple for them. This is why there are so many folk tales about distressed spirits who only needed to correct or say this one thing and were suddenly settled.

Whatever these people need of you to find their peace, this is not just a benevolent endeavour. If these people are your true ancestors your well-being is directly linked with theirs and numerous sources of ill luck or disharmony that have been your lot since you can remember are linked to the inherited presence of their dis-ease. When they settle, and the dead sigh an out-breath of appeasement, whole cities rest easier.

Do remember, however, that dead people who are themselves stuck in some kind of repetitive behaviour will often try to pull you into their loop; trying to pull you into entering, and hopefully not leaving, their psycho-drama. You must prove you can resist this and that your will is stronger than theirs before you will be able to work with them. You must remain the one who is grounded, anchored and calmly insistent the work be completed. If your dead overrun you, setting themselves up as demi-gods in your life and begin to manipulate you to play out their dramas (whether that be their alcoholism or their hatred of men) this early in your journey, then this is definitely a sign you aren't ready yet.

Moon 9

The Seasons of Life

> Time is a sensible dimension in the realm of the spirits. It is as sensible a dimension in the spirit realm as length, breadth, and thickness are sensible dimensions to those of us who still live and breathe on Earth. Time is the principal dimension of the physical universe, as it is the dimension along which we move. A spirit, in the realm of the spirits, can see your development approaching in the same way that you can see an approaching automobile on a highway. It is nothing for a powerful spirit to wait patiently as you develop yourself, in the same way that you might wait for a friend to pick you up in his automobile.
> (Martin Coleman)

One of the things most rewarding about practising a form of

magic that involves ancestry and the magic of the body is the perspective it gives you on the life cycle. Having left behind our bundle of cultural conditioning, it is likely we will find ourselves questioning received wisdom regarding maturation and old age. Once you start meeting serious practitioners of the art magical you may meet some very old individuals dwelling in young bodies, and some eternally young ones whose daylight body is showing signs of age.

If you're a witchcraft practitioner, or someone who associates with the title 'witch' in some way, there is a special onus on you to be specifically aware and ruthless with pruning this condition. The power in the hag figure of the witch cannot be overstated. This figure is not just powerful because she's old, or because she has accumulated wisdom, or because women in particular are witches in some biological way linked to the cycles of their reproductive systems ... But because she is all of us, she is the image of the most reviled and least valued type of body. The female body when it is no longer fertile. In this way the hag is always the appropriate symbol of the witch, for she is the one most free of living up to society's expectations of beauty and utility.

She is as much a symbol for male practitioners as she is for women, for when the fullness of forms is understood and ancestral material is unpacked all begin to discover these potentialities in ourselves and the way our own bodies have been oppressed and vilified through what was done to the bodies of our mothers and grandmothers. Young women carry the trauma encoded into them of young men who fought in terrible wars and became their grandfathers. Young men carry in them the rapes and the abuse of generations of their foremothers. None of us are unharmed by the harm that has been done. The only difference is that for some groupings this trauma is explicit and remembered and for others it sits below the waterline.

For this reason the ancestral work we have begun will extend into this moon. It is that important. As we delve deeper into the magical implications of the stages of life we will find we already have the potential for inherent knowledge of old age, even if we haven't experienced it yet. We will have to deal with the feelings of resistance that will come up around that. Many spiritual traditions speak of dealing with the inner child, but here we must also access our future elder. Our vision of them will be skewed by the fog created by our ancestors' traumas, and by our own trauma received via inadequate modelling of the ageing process.

Ever since I was little the women in my family have been talking about ageing. My mother would tell me about ways to rub cream into your face to prevent future wrinkles when I was still ten years old. Regularly I would hear them criticise their own appearance along the basis of age, describing their body in unfairly negative terms. I realise now that given the age my mother was when I was born, these people were only about the age I am now when this was occurring.

For me personally age, or 'ageing' is not a thing I've had much experience with yet. I know I'm maturing with the passage of years but my worldview is so radically different that the thought of running myself down in front of my children as old, as both physically over the hill and culturally out of touch, as I experienced my parents doing while I was growing up, has just not occurred to me. Whether this attitude means I am in fact just not ageing as quickly I don't know, but it has certainly been said about witches that they don't age the same as other people. Some people think this has to do with the fat of unbaptised infants we use as face creams.

Regardless of opinion or rumour, all agree that not ageing has something to do with the face, the daylight body's outer skin that so much weight is placed upon. This burden the single image of the self must carry is heavy enough to weigh anyone to earth more rapidly! Those who live in the fullness of their forms don't have to bear that weight and so their spirit occupies a space with a certain lightness of being. They don't think stiffly, they don't acquire calcified worldviews that resist change, and so in some way, even though they eventually get wrinkles in their daylight skin like every other thing exposed to air, they maintain a youthful suppleness. Many a canny witch has discovered this old trick. There is more to anointing the face with the dew of the May Blossom in the pre-dawn hours to maintain one's youth than meets the eye. This is about exposing all of your faces, the soul essence that animates them all, to the quintessence of newness. It is to wash clear the face of our daimon so it may shine forth to visible manifestation in our daylight face.

What is less understood about navigating age is that the same is true in the opposite direction. Because we live in a world that has an obsession with the appearance of youth, this magic of imbibing youth is far more appealing than the magic of imbibing age when you are yet still young ... Yet the secret of avoiding the negative modelling of old age you have probably encountered so often you're now afraid of it, lies in coming at the matter from both directions. If you can do that now you will be ensuring not only powerful magical practice in the present, but a strong current of productive occult work all the way up until your most senior years.

Before we launch into the work for this moon I'd like to discuss a bit about the rituals of life that most of us have lost. If you're reading this book to prepare yourself for entry, or as a kind of detox whilst involved in a tradition that provides rituals for the life cycle then you are very lucky. Everybody else might have to do some research and reach back into the ancestral memory of their forebears to begin honouring these threshold moments again. Most modern magical groups fall into one of two categories, covens of people who split up far too soon to have experienced all the important life marking moments together, and occult lodges that don't really touch on those kinds of domestic concerns that happen outside the circle. I am fortunate enough to belong to a tradition to which neither of those things applies, and it is from that perspective I am writing here.

The first thing you might need to do is check if you recognise yourself in this exchange between my characters in *Wooing the Echo*:

> 'What are you? Working class? Middle class? You've got no county accent so you went to a good school.'
>
> Christopher felt utterly taken aback at this brutally honest discussion of class, something that he'd always experienced as a kind of taboo subject.
>
> 'Yes, I went to Bishops after a Steiner school, so I guess we are very middle class. I live in one of those newer houses near the Long Barrow. It's two storied with plush carpets and air-conditioning. It has three bathrooms and even the towel rack is heated. Everything I wear smells like fake lavender from my mum's fabric softener,' Christopher declared with a passionate hatred that even he hadn't expected from himself.
>
> Seth surprised him then by laughing. It was a genuinely happy sound, a new softer sound that was endearing to Christopher.
>
> 'And you are not happy with your environment then?' he asked, beginning to roll himself a cigarette.
>
> Christopher smiled. 'You could say that.'
>
> 'For someone who's had such a fill of all things modern you sure aren't anything special with cars.'
>
> Christopher laughed. 'I've never been the car kind of boy.'
>
> 'You bookish?' Seth asked, licking the edge of his cigarette paper.
>
> 'Yes, intensely.'
>
> 'You don't look bookish.'
>
> 'No, that's part of my dilemma.'
>
> 'Ah,' said Seth. With a smile he placed the cigarette between his lips and lit it. 'I thought there was a dilemma. What is it?'

'I suppose that it's just that I'm bookish, and weird. But my body wants to do other things. I feel all out of place.'

Seth nodded to himself as he smoked. 'Are you a virgin?'

Christopher tried not to show his shock or his sudden embarrassment at something that had not previously embarrassed him. 'Yes.'

'Ever killed anything you ate?'

'No.'

'Ever seen anything born, human or animal? Eaten anything you saw die or made anything you use from scratch?'

'No for all.'

'Simple case of "Male, Middle Class and White Syndrome".'

Christopher winced; Seth's words were so true they were painful.

Of course the fact Christopher is male and white could easily be otherwise and this same life story could apply (except perhaps for the virginity detail, which is somewhat rarer). The point is that he's a young man feeling alienated, looking for answers outside the box and the hedge, but he hasn't even experienced the life cycle vicariously yet, even via animals ... It is shocking how many adults have never seen a human born or die, and in some cases for younger people they haven't even seen these things happen to animals. Let alone having killed an animal for food, despite having eaten many.

These kinds of confrontations with responsibility and intensity are a kind of conversation with reality that many of us just don't get to have enough of, and when we do they are seldom well managed in the way we're exposed to them. They lack the sanctity of cross-over rituals. If there is one major and ongoing lifestyle choice that you decide to keep on the back of this thirteen moon project, I would strongly suggest the following: seek out life situations that will allow you to have these life experiences. Try to live closer to the life processes of birth, sexuality and death in as many ways as you can. This will grow your spiritual maturity in the way manure grows plants.

The next step is to think about how you honour the sanctity of these important marking stones in life on your own journey. Do you have a ritual for a baby's first bath? What should be done with the afterbirth? Do you have coming of age rituals for honouring the onset of adulthood? How will you acknowledge events like the cessation of the menses? I especially want you to put cross-gender (if that idea is even relevant to how you see the world) thought into these questions. For women to think about rites for a boy's coming of age and men to think about things like the magical significance of the menopause. The latter will be of great importance because society has traditionally tabooed male interest in women's lives as a sign of some kind of lack of masculinity. Some women may find doing the opposite confronting for other reasons, such as it bringing up repressed anger. If you are exclusively homosexual in orientation you might think that childbirth has nothing to do with you, and I'd like you to confront this thought in the same manner. You yourself were born, and we must try to see everything that happens in every stage and shape of the body of mankind with the same importance and level of interest. In this way we can push beyond the narrow confines of our mortal shape and current age into the territory of strange ancestral atavisms and greater identification with what we perceive as Other.

In a lot of manifestations of modern paganism you see the Goddess defined as three-fold, a Maiden, Mother and a Crone. Some men involved with this kind of witchcraft or paganism respond by designating their own threefold life experience, the human version being seen as following that of the goddess and god narrative. Here I would like to point out that in the kind of witchcraft I practise, the role of 'crone' is quite unsuitable to the post-menopausal woman. There is about another twenty years in the middle that desperately requires a new story. This is the time of a new heat and warrior-drive, fiery like the leaves of autumn, a good time for enjoying the fruits of one's labours, as well as making preparations for winter. To rush straight to winter because summer is over merely shows how little use or value our culture can imagine for a non-breeding female. I say this instead of 'infertile' in inverted commas because in a magical sense this old bodily fertility turns inward towards a flowering of the spirit-as-flesh. The threefold goddess idea places such emphasis on birthing capacity that you'd think as soon as it was gone you instantly transform into an ancient crone.

Now, if you are yourself a woman or experienced through your mother the generational conditioning around age you will probably notice in yourself a certain resistance to these thoughts. They might sound something like: *it's a beautiful idea but the world isn't like that. All the postmenopausal women I know are hormonal and bitter and upset about hot flashes all the time.* Or: *all right for you to say!* Or something along those lines. If you were raised a boy you probably also heard your own messages about when your usefulness will expire. You probably have at least once looked at elderly men in states of helpless debility and quickly looked away lest the horror of their vulnerability play on your mind. Masculinity is framed in mainstream culture as never being vulnerable, and yet we all know this awaits us, and if we thought about it more may treat the vulnerable differently. Somewhere in us we all know there is a potential elderly person who could one day be as they are. Some of us will meet this idea by resolving to control their own death in some way, saying they plan to smoke or take a lot of drugs so they don't live too long and laughing off the uncomfortable spectre of your own future old man.

Instead, I'd like you to give some long and hard thought to where you heard everything that set up your view of what it was to age? Who used to talk to you about it and what did they say? What, if any, positive views of old age and the stages of maturation that lead up to it were you supplied with? Did you also see concrete examples of useful, vigorous, or just simply wise elders from an early age, people you could see as inspiring examples of how one could grow old with grace or simply spectacularly? If you find you have almost no memories of any of the latter positive modelling, I would suggest you begin by doing a web search of inspiring older people in different fields of interest you hold, so you can counterbalance the negative messages. Read as much as you can find that is actually written by intelligent and driven elderly people (preferably those of seventy) about the experience of getting older and just about their perspective on their trade, art or area of expertise and how it has progressed with them through the years. Pay attention to any prejudices you might notice in yourself as a result of your early conditioning.

If you are yourself an older person, I would like you to do the opposite. Purposely look for the work and educated opinions of young, dynamic and talented Millennials and Gen Z folk. Recognise their unique voice as a generation and try not to judge it for not being the same as your own. Consider life from the perspective of a Millennial. Keep in mind that they grew up with the Internet and that the vast majority of their generation has grown up acknowledging that climate change is real and will most likely seriously disrupt this civilisation after you are dead and they are not. If you find this difficult you need only compare these things to issues that were happening when you were young, such as growing up with television or the threat of nuclear war, which may not have been issues for your parents. As you will probably remember, if you allow yourself to enter a true reverie, there were things about growing up in that time that your parents just couldn't possibly understand. Now you stand where they stood. How do you plan to conduct yourself?

As Kahlil Gibran put it when it comes to the next generation:

> You may house their bodies but not their souls, for their souls dwell in the house of tomorrow, which you cannot visit, not even in your dreams. You may strive to be like them, but seek not to make them like you. For life goes not backward nor tarries with yesterday. You are the bows from which your children as living arrows are sent forth. The archer sees the mark upon the path of the infinite, and He bends you with His might that His arrows may go swift and far.

Having been in the position to read this quote both as an arrow and a bow, I know very well that it was an uplifting thought when I was the arrow and a more austere sort of joy when I realised I was now the bow. But there is a great grace available to us all in allowing that role to come over us, whilst at the same time knowing we are still simultaneously on our own arrow path flying forth from our own parents' bow.

In many ways the most complex time is in the middle between these two extremes. It is the time (the age will vary depending on when and if you had children or dependents) where I am now in life; I have children that I must be a steady bow for but am still very much an arrow flying forth from my parents' generation, with no real hope of being able to relinquish either role any time soon. There is a grace available here too, in the middle of maelstrom, a Janus-headed vision in both directions. You are still able to relate to youth culture but becoming increasingly empathic to the experience of older people also. Part of you is still in flight, still finding your life's purpose and the other part of you is laying itself down as a king makes a bridge of himself, for those younger and more vulnerable to crossover. If this description brings tears to your eyes, and so does the Gibran quote, you will know you are either being someone's bridge right now, or you remember what it was to lie down everything to make a bedrock for someone else's future.

This moon, I'd like you to purchase two writing notebooks and designate one for yourself as a youth and one for yourself as an elder. As you sit before the blank book that is to be filled with a story about your younger self, meditate before you do anything on its blankness. Like this empty book, your dropping of your bundle has emptied this space. Whatever childhood photographs your parents keep of you, tell this person that the one they raised and who was shaped by society, has died. This stark fact should be considered as you leaf through the white pages. Luckily for your parents they aren't aware of it, they will likely continue to conduct a relationship with the shade of that person for the remainder of their days. To some extent you could say that many human relationships follow this pattern. But you are the anomaly in your family line, the blip, the mutant gene, the one who is going to turn it all on its head and do things differently. You're going to imagine a different story.

Think about who you truly were as a child, what native impulses moved you and shone through you? What was the shape of your soul which your family and society trimmed the edges off and twisted into another form? I want you to write something about who you were as a young person that goes back in time and re-writes your story of your early self. The backstory that belongs to the person you have chosen to be today, your authentic self. To help you to more deeply comprehend the task, I'm going to include Frater A's testimonial as an example of how deep this work can be.

> When I was a young fellow I came from a family of very talented individuals: artists, talented barristers, musicians, photographers and natural scientists. I was given a lot of opportunity to try different things as hobbies, but the direction my employment was to follow was set out for me. There was no getting out of that. I was the oldest son and so I would carry on the family legal practice. I often thought

about what I might have otherwise done … The thing was I was always a polymath, interested and passionate about a great number of things. I had a suitably pleasant singing voice as a child that became a passable tenor at manhood, I could play a little music on a couple of instruments but I was never greatly gifted at it, I could draw and paint but I was nothing special, I did well at maths and debating and saw them as a mental game. I collected samples and fossils and loved natural sciences and geography, anthropology, I loved the visual arts, above nearly everything on earth loved poetry. I loved passion and anyone who was crazy about what they did to the point of obsession. I loved beautiful things, both the symmetrical and perfect and the things others might term deformed or savage. I loved animals, landscape photography, hiking and travel, collection and curating, rules and regulations and people who broke all the rules and regulations … It seemed like there were too many options, too many potential paths, so it was easier to let my family take over and decide for me. The reality I see now very clearly is that the real talent I had was that I love things. Love is my talent, seeing beauty in and loving things is my real gift, the core of who I am. If I had known that when I was a boy and young man ... If I'd known that one simple fact and that it was what made me special and that I must not let anyone devalue it … Well, life would have worked out a lot differently, let me put it that way. Once I'd realised that and removed from my person all the head-ducking to authority and the shaming of my natural impulses it made it pretty easy to write something about what that boy was like. I laughed as I wrote about him and his deeds and misdeeds. What a firecracker he was! The things he did! The risks he took … Now you might think this would incline one to regret and dwelling on bitterness but I look at it in a more Quantum, multiple versions of reality kind of way. Somewhere out there in a parallel history of myself,

> that boy existed. So I choose to draw power from his exploits and to increase my confidence by relating to his story more than the reality my parents or contemporaries would have told you about my history. This is one of the ways my occult practice has empowered me to move forward as someone no longer defined by his mistakes. I am no longer the result of my ordinary history, but my extraordinary history.

Don't stop writing his or her story for at least half of the month. Come back to this notebook over the entire waxing of the moon and continue to write down anecdotes and histories from the life and adventures of this new authentic you-as-youth. You will begin to see that this youthful you is not just you without the restrictions of society and family, but also in some ways personifies the spirit of Youth itself. When you are writing, if you put yourself into the story enough, you might feel this quick, greenish current of life force coursing through you. Remember that time is a sensible dimension in the Otherworld, so it is always possible to look backwards at it and project your current power in both directions, towards the true essence of who you have always been as a child, and toward the potential you who will one day become an elder.

Once you have reached the waning of the moon it is time to take out the other blank notebook. Contemplate the emptiness of the book again. It doesn't matter whether you are a very long way from being an elder or already there in years, I would like you to consider it as an unwritten book in just the same manner. Because who you were set out to be had you stayed within the hedge and not dropped your bundle is not who you are now fated to become. If you strip away all the negative voices telling you that an older person is less attractive, what would you really see in the mirror? Lines that tell tales of character, joy and suffering … This same kind of rugged beauty is often appreciated in the landscape, but not in the landscape of the body. Mainstream society is more interested in what you produce at a material level than your soul and wisdom, so we can happily discard its input. We also have a variety of other forms, such as the youth whose true story we have spent the waxing moon writing.

What could you as an elder be like? Knowing as you do what you know now? Knowing where the world bent you out of shape as a child? Having re-storied that experience and written a new story of your life that more properly fits who you've decided to become, who could this person become? Remember the sky is the limit, but you need to be able to conceptualise this person first, before you can become them. This may require you to face ancestral blocks made up by many generations of people who yielded to the same limitations about what being an elder could mean for them.

To open up other options for your future potentiality you will need to ask present-day-you the right questions. We are inclined to ask ourselves who we want to be and what we want to achieve but ask yourself also: whom or what do you serve as an elder? Don't be narrow in your answer and assume things like 'children' or 'grand-children'. What about political movements? What about LGBT youth? What about helping other elder folks to come into their power and remain supple and adaptive to a scary, changing world? What about the land itself? What about spiritual as well as biological progeny? If part of your vision of whom you serve as elder is your physical descendants, then how does this future-you make them a strong bow to send forth arrows into their future? What strategies does he or she discover that allow this grace and strength to be maintained?

Don't just make elder-you a series of achievements but write anecdotes from their life also, as you did with yourself as a youth. Put them into stories, exciting or beautiful stories that model the kind of person you are incubating inside yourself, slowly becoming, and send power to the realisation of that person. We are inclined to think we have to hurry to do all the good things in life while we are still 'young enough to enjoy it' but there are some forms of appreciation that increase as we mature and become more piquant. Think about some forms of acquired tastes that you didn't enjoy until recently in your life, what are some others you haven't acquired yet that elder-you now knows about and enjoys? Send love and respect to elder-you, for they are the fruition of your life's work taking shape to form your final personal and occult legacy.

Moon 10

Sexing Magic

You don't have to go mad to see them, but you must abandon reason to keep them around after the sight. Giants, nymphs, ghosts—they're there, you've seen them maybe once but then looked away and forgot. Shaking off and away the vision, looking again, changing your view so they're not there on the second glance. Dis-enchanted. We don't do this just with the Other, we do this with ourselves, particularly with desire. The Other is queer, sometimes we are, and like the man denying desire for another man in a world where only women are allowed, the Other is the queer we disallow. Easier to deny different desire when surrounded by others who also deny; easier to disallow god-giants when no-one else admits to them. To dis-allow is to forbid; to dis-enchant is to de-ny, repudiate, withhold from ourselves what we thought

> occurred. Self-abnegation, sacrificial poverty of spirit so we can be what we're supposed to be, what is demanded of us. Resist the trembling lust for what your flesh desires and no thing queer enters into the world of self-controlled workers selling time for money.
> (Rhyd Wildermuth, 'Awakening The Land')

There is probably not a part of the Western psyche more deeply damaged than the parts relating to sex and gender. When you start off everything as an either/or proposition it's almost inevitable that one of those two propositions tends to carry a hierarchical weight imbalance. Nature gave about half of us vaginas, and the other almost half of us penises, and a small minority of us something in-between. Those sexual differences come with relatively standard physical differences regarding hair growth and muscle/fat distribution, we as humans gave ourselves the stories about what those differences *meant.*

If we choose to accept the idea that there is no one overarching and divinely ordained story about what it means to be made in these different shapes, then we have a much greater chance of having experiences outside our previous reality tunnel. Please consider going back and reading that sentence again. This isn't just about trying to convince you to abandon your comfortable ideas about gender or to adopt some radical political stance; this is about trying to open your future up to the widest number of possible outcomes. The more possibilities you're shut down to, the less ways your magic will be able to take effect, so this is simply a pragmatic decision.

Any preconceived notion that sorts people into categories and assigns a universal meaning to that category was meant to go into your bundle. But that doesn't mean you aren't still carrying it without realising, this is why the final moon is called *Rinse and Repeat*! If you have previously belonged to a mystical or religious ideology that posits certain meanings behind an eternal feminine and eternal masculine principle, you may feel defensive about my suggestions here.

If you do that's a good thing, it means you've discovered some resistance to starting again that you probably weren't aware of, part of you has adhered itself to a doctrine and feels threatened when that doctrine is threatened. That's natural, as no one can be without a ruling perspective of some kind, we as occultists just want to make sure we choose the most effective and flexible worldview that gives us the greatest scope for empowerment and to create personal change when we need to. People who get backed into tight corners are often so ideologically bound that from their perspective there is genuinely no way out and no solution because there are only so many possible ways for them to act or think within their framework. If they could change that framework, multiple options that could be sorcerously exploited would reveal themselves.

So perhaps if the concept of abolishing these categories entirely makes you uncomfortable because your whole spiritual worldview rests on a concept of gendered polarities, just consider it a mental exercise or game for now, something you plan to try on for size. You don't have to adhere to any specific way of thinking; you can just consider this one as an exercise in perspective shifting.

Imagine that there is no universal masculine or feminine and that mankind has projected his own culturally dictated ideas on the universe, designating the certain things like the sun as masculine, and other things like the moon, as feminine. What would happen if, rather than taking this as another article of faith we just agreed to drop all of it and see what it feels like from the inside? What is it like to have testosterone as a strong force in your body like a grown man does, but to feel it without calling it things, without categorizing it with certain words or behaviours, but to just know that feeling viscerally, wordlessly? I think anyone who's had a standard-male level of testosterone in their body will agree with me that it has a feeling of sorts, a signature if you will; you only have to remember back to it firing up at puberty to get a sense of its energy. But for gods' sake, for once, let us not name it things just yet; let us not pile words on top of the feeling for awhile. Just sit with it. To sit and stop talking about what it means to be a man and making lists of how it means this thing because it's the opposite of being a woman, and actually *be with it* outside of words. We don't have to do this with society breathing down our necks, we don't have to perform it on social media; we can do it alone in our room.

What would it feel like to be an estrogen and progesterone empowered body without the labels about femininity and the historical burden many hear along with the word 'woman'? What if we could let the body be without all these words, tables, theories and binaries, just for a time? What voices that are now a whisper would become a scream? I hear a lot of people like to claim they are empowered by their tradition or their ideology's idea of what it means to be a woman, or what it means to be a man, yet I am highly sceptical that ideas ever empower the body, only the ego. And what is vital and pre-verbal of whatever that sense of being in your sexed body means to you will still be there after you've tried this, as nothing which is truly real need fear removal, nothing real may be lost.

These are red-button issues for a reason. People are hurt in these places and there are few good words that can be said about them for this reason. All the words are laden with something, polluted at their life-stream with prejudice and anger against prejudice, and finally by anger, about anger, about prejudice and so on ... This is why I say the true wisdom that is left lies in silent experience beyond words, beyond labels, even the comforting kinds.

Here my saying is relevant: don't look the Medusa directly in the face. In this context the Medusa is the entire knot or problem that we as humans have created out of sex and gender, things that never really needed to be problems. Engaging with the argument on its own terms is to look the Medusa in the face, then everything turns to stone, you end up with opposing camps with fixed, very loud attitudes about something that is better off being wordless and existing in the flux of bodily experience.

Finding a way to circumnavigate around the problem and thus un-see it as a problem, is more like using a mirror to see where the Medusa is located. So this is what we're going to do. Instead of arguing about what it means to practise male or female mysteries and to what extent sex can safely be used in magic without abuse and all the other very vexed and emotive questions that surround this topic we are going to do what we were asked to do in Leaving the Bundle, and step right outside the whole thing, and deeper inside our embodied experience.

Choose a time and space where you can be alone and uninterrupted. If it can be arranged, have your room suitably warm so that you can be naked without discomfort. If there are any mirrors or reflective surfaces likely to be visible cover them over, we do not wish to get stuck in the reductive image of the self and for it to stand between us and the direct experience of the body. Make yourself comfortable either supine or in another comfortable posture. I want you to create an elaborate mental fiction for yourself. Convince yourself that you've never heard of a meaning being ascribed to being male or female, that you've never heard of gay or straight that you've never heard of any lower value being given to being male or female, to the body or to the sex itself. Imagine, in fact, that your body is a body without history of oppression by the intellect, as if it has not been flagellated with ideas and made to conform to them. That it has not been taught it must be one thing in opposition to some other thing that it could just *be* and *experience* and *sense* freely.

What feelings move across the surface of your skin in response to these thoughts? What currents of power move under the skin? What are the body's nameless desires? All of them, inside and outside the old categories. What are its inclinations in this moment? Does it want to move? Is it becoming aroused, fuelled and engorged with blood just by the heady sense of its liberation from the prison of ideology? Respond to your body's wants in whatever way is natural to you without thoughts of why it should be right or wrong to do so and what certain schools of thought think about sexual release of this kind or that kind … Let all the chatter die off. You will realise quite how much is chatter …

As you realise you don't have to explain, apologise or even name your body's urges to anyone, to fit them into your politics or social schema, they can be just that, an inexplicable and untame urge arising from the many bodies' own atavistic intelligences, there is a realisation of your bodies as a site of freedom. The site, as we have said, is of continuous revolution. Unless you choose to involve someone else you don't have to ask 'may I' of creed or doctrine, your body of flesh and blood knowing can answer the questions for you of what is good for it, what feels good, what brings good … As long as you can learn to listen to it and honour what it truly needs. We often mistake what our consciousness needs for the needs of our body. Addiction doesn't ever result from the needs or wants of a healthy body, but from a mind and heart in need of solace. We tend to blame the body for wanting this or that and project our less healthy behaviours as our body's wants without even asking. This space during this tenth moon is about *asking*.

What you discover about yourself doesn't necessarily require the crafting of a new socially-collaborated identity around it, though perhaps in time it could lead that way. Hopefully if it does it will be a more flexible identity that gives you room to move, if your sexuality and bodily sense of gender requires it. But it is best if you allow a certain fertile silence for a time afterwards, not immediately naming or restricting the newcomer in the flesh with names or titles, let alone exposing this one who is feeling from inside you to the glare of public opinion. What the public thinks of or how it defines this one you are feeling as, or these ones, should never again be a central lens through which your body or sex is experienced.

The practice described above is designed to regain ownership over the holy body. The body is being reclaimed here as a form of intelligence in its own right, rather than inert matter dominated by a brain or even ethical system. For those who lead from an ethical centre are often in such a hurry to ascribe right or wrong to things that they spend no time on what the body wants, only ascribing the things to it they believe it is right it should want. Many who haven't yet heard the voice of the tabernacle of the flesh are filled with many fears about what would happen if they listened to this voice. But the truth is, the consequences of the many returns of the repressed that the ignored fetch and inherent sensuality of the body visits upon us for our efforts is far worse by way of any perversity that can be imagined, than any of the innocent desires of what Mary Oliver terms 'the warm, soft animal of the body'.

When it comes to experiencing sex and the fullness of forms we would do well to listen to Judith Butler as well, who also said: 'Lets face it. We are undone by each other. And if we're not, we're missing something.' In short, this will not be easy. To find a lover that can perceive and love you in your fullness of forms, the youth in you through to the elder, the animal nature/s and every other gender or form that rises to your surface skin is finding a true pearl.

But you are either an occultist already or priming yourself to become one, so you are no doubt a patient pearl fisherman. You know better than to give up or set something you want as impossible. If you are not interested in this experience then in one way you will save yourself a lot of effort and heartache, but you may need to find other non-sexual ways to experience Being Seen. Because during intimacy there is a strong opportunity for the many skins and faces of a person to rise to the surface and the strong vibration of openness and pleasure usually makes it easier for them to be seen.

This being said, there is no right way to go about exploring your body's desires, they may not even focus on genital sexuality. We are here to listen to our body, not tell it that it is something, whether what you're telling it must be is sexual or asexual, either is a crime against it if you are doing it without its full consent. So listen, and when you have listened, honour your body's wishes. It may be the first time that either you or anyone else has ever fully done so. Purposely block out all the voices telling you you're doing it wrong even though it's none of their damned business anyway.

If you do find yourself working alone (and this should be practised by people who wish to engage in magically charged sexuality with others as well) you should try fantasizing about sex in your different bodies. Visualise yourself engaging sexually with a wide range of Other bodies, people older or younger than yourself, angels, goblins, gods, were-beasts, you yourself will be in different animal skins or monster forms of all sorts. Lean into sensations you find challenging and interesting with the mindset of experimentation rather than letting the heaviness with which this culture views sexuality into the equation. Think about all that weight you are sloughing off. The morality police even outside the church have their insidious shaming strategies about what one should or should not even be allowed to masturbate about, long before we even talk about what happens between two or more consenting adults! Nobody owns inside your head, or the impulses of your flesh. They only get a say if you are asking them to get involved in some way.

Many people who've been trained in other occult or mystical schools that utilize sex will immediately become suspicious of magical intrusion or vampiric entities drawing off their sexual force and using the visualised forms to get access to your life force etc. These will often be the same people who will tell you that internet porn is slowly building massive egregores of masturbation energy all aimed at something very negative. Now once again I'm going to ask you for something a bit radical, for the time being just don't worry about it. Don't worry about whether this school or that believes this or that about ejaculation or intercourse with spirits or thought-forms ... Just be with your bodies, stretch your wings and claws and reach out to the unseen with animal purity of heart.

The thing you will often find is that most of the heavy, parasitic entities that can be observed swarming over some forms of sexual activities are attracted by the collective hang-ups and anxieties (i.e. worrying) of mankind rather than caused by the sex itself. The hang-up provides a kind of fissure in the energy field of the person, for want of a better term, through which the raw life force of sexuality can be accessed for predation. This is why individuals who are badly ridden by such forces (human sexual predators) want to not only touch their victims against their will but to shame them and make them feel dirty as well. A prime example is the way that women are both pursued sexually and shamed for being sluts, often by the same person. This sort of behaviour makes perfect sense for the parasite but makes little sense for a person wanting more sex from women. One is surely likely to get more sex with women if one doesn't shame them for liking sex!

You will notice that I try to keep saying things over and over like 'men do this'. The reason for this evasion is another example of not looking the Medusa directly in the eye. To affirm with my words that a certain group is a certain way is to give power to the parasite. It is to say I surrender to acknowledging its presence in all men. This isn't a little nicety solely for people who identify as male but a positive step taken in the direction of hope for all people, as girls and women are deeply affected by the mental health of boys and men. Shame is the number one way that our outer defences are broken through. If we shame an individual with the actions of a group we make them more vulnerable to becoming part of the problem. We have made a resolution in ourselves to Step Out from thinking from inside categories and labels and we must therefore try to meet other individuals as just that.

When you achieve the kind of Edenic innocence state aimed for over this moon, where your body is finally alone in its senses, finally separate from all the angry voices of the world screaming its opinions at it about its aesthetic value and the value of its sexual urges, you are safe in the same way that toddlers seldom hurt themselves when they fall. If anything does go wrong and something leaves you feeling unwell or dispirited, apply the cleansing baths and powders provided earlier, and every time you practise, surround the area with such incenses and waters as are bane to parasites, or work inside a circle.

When or if you do get involved with someone sexually and you wish to include them in understanding you at a magical level, this is how I would be inclined to go about it. Think of your expanded perception of reality as a bit like a kind of kink. Your partner will have to understand what it is you like about it before they are likely to want to try it with you.

The best first step is to ask them if they'd be willing to read this book. Even if they don't subscribe to a magical worldview they might be willing to take part in this chapter with you at an imaginative level, when considered as a kind of mental role-playing game. Any casual look at adult dating sites geared towards BDSM and fetish will tell you that there are far more abstract and idiosyncratic turn-ons that some people have! In the scheme of the weird and wonderful world of unrepressed human sexuality, the idea that you have other hidden bodies and subtle forms that can have sex in multiple ways is hardly that unusual. Below I have included something I've written about my own ecstatic sex experiences.

His green devil-eyes glimmered with undeniable charisma as he peeked out from behind the standing stone that now stood where my Shadow had been. His eyes seemed to taunt me, draw me to some realisation that still lay beyond him. Sometimes I wanted to shake him or slap him. All of a sudden he was standing in front of the standing stone, leaning casually against it. His posture looked like that of a young man who might start whistling to himself or light up a smoke.

But he didn't light up a cigarette, he took out a knife and came toward me. I didn't feel afraid. I had faced too many horrors before, as I stumbled and fell and tore my flesh on the briar roses, along this Crooked and Time-Rutted Path. He had been my tender murderer before, the dead have nothing to fear from knives.

Instead he presented me with the hilt, and looking at him with some confusion I took the blade from him. It was clear to me without him needing to speak to me that he meant for me to plunge the dagger into him. Immediately I was shaking my head.

'I can't do that!'

He was closer now, my hands were in his. As always I trembled with excitement at his proximity. Thanks to him I had some idea that the nature of Heaven on Earth lay in this experience, where everything is always renewing itself and every familiar thing remains a wonder.

'But you must.' He smiled.

It was almost impossible to say 'no' to him when he smiled like that. People who talk about 'the charm of the devil' know what they are talking about.

'For me,' he added, 'I need you to set me free! Don't you see?' he whispered with great intensity, 'This is your test of Love. If you love me you'll kill this form you've trapped me in.'

I frowned then with great consternation.

'I've trapped you?' The idea appalled me. But he was still smiling.

'Not exactly. But you've trapped yourself. Do it if you love me.'

I gripped the dagger tightly in my hand, but I was shaking. Anyone who knows me, really knows me and what I am capable of when the beautiful abomination of Love is upon me, will know that I did it. But first before I did I asked him,

'Are you a part of me?'

'Don't limit me.'

'Are you separate from me?'

'Don't limit me.'

'Are you human?'

'Don't limit me.'

Smiling again.

'Are you a god?'

'Sometimes ...'

He gave the Sign of Silence then. And I heard his voice in my head again: sacrifice your words for things, and then you'll see how we can be together. All your Desire is Me.

I struck then. I think it's fair to say that it was harder than the Mystery of My Own Death, as enacted at a different crossroads. He bled human blood, heart's blood. And the familiar image I had come to Know of him fell away like dust.

Beneath that Spirit-Skin ... How can human words configure Him? I wanted to fall to my knees with awe and lust, and yet he held me there.

There were the golden goat's horns that erupted from his brow, the light that shone from his brow and the pinkened skin around the heat of it. From the waist down he was satyr like, hairy and dark and from the waist up he was an angel. There was a peacock iridescence in his eyes and occasionally dancing over the skin of his face.

'Witch-Father ...' I whispered.

And yet there also was the man, the daemon, that I had loved for countless lifetimes. For truly he wasn't all lying (although he is the Father of them) when he said 'yes I've been a man.' And in the eyes of Man that were there among the other things I saw traces of every man I'd ever loved. And the women too, for he was not limited in this way.

He took my head in his hands then and brought me close. As our brows touched I felt my own form begin to morph and shift. From my contorted back erupted the strange leathery wings of the bat, and my head leaked snakes until all my hair was as the hair of the Medusa. My feet that clutched at his thighs were the talons of birds and I was both-sexed.

When he bent me over a flatter standing stone that had not been there before to take me from behind, I felt temporarily disappointed. I wanted to look upon his brilliant, freakish beauty. But the faces started pressing and bubbling under my skin then, rising to the surface so you could see the shape of them under my skin. They were other men I'd been, other women, ancestor-women who live along the red-threads of my flesh. They were one tumult of Desire for Him, they too were in my Desire, my Desire was Universal, a transpersonal force of Nature.

One of the faces broke free just below my tailbone, a terrible bone-cracking, flesh-flower of pain, as if I'd given birth to it. And yet now I was seeing in two directions at once. Through my own eyes and with the set of eyes that had appeared in this nether-face. He kissed the mouth of the Other, the Woman Under the Flesh, like he'd always known she was in there and had been waiting. And then he fed his cock into her mouth.

I realised then in the inferno of my brain that I was unlimited by all constraints. So I twisted my spine all the way around until I was facing him and my legs were facing backward. The faces continued to undulate under my skin and my bat wings enveloped us, so that we were one writhing creature made up of human, goat, snake, bat and flame parts. He placed our foreheads together.

That's when I saw the Sabbat of the Three-Way Crossroads, the Infernal, Earthly and Celestial Sabbats all made one. And it had been there all along! There were other creatures like us everywhere, many of them conjoined as we were, some of them in even more complex combinations with more entities involved. I truly knew no limitation for I was a part of the Two-Backed-Beast and yet I was walking in another Skin among them, both at the same time.

I saw witches in horned masks, in green-man masks, masks with hare's faces, or upturned crescent moons upon the brow. I saw witches with one mask on the front of their head and one on the back so you couldn't tell which way they were looking. Many of them stopped on the other side of the fire in the centre to regard me. Their movements seemed so light as they danced and cavorted that they were eerie, and when they stopped stock still they were even more so.

I realised then that I had no mask on. And as though they heard my thoughts one of them that I thought may have been a woman, approached me. She wore the mask of a hare, and very slowly, so slowly that it was entrancing to watch, unmasked herself before me. Instead of a face I saw nothing but a glowing skeleton. The skeleton laughed, threw back its mantle and began to dance wildly. And though I knew that there was divinity in these masks I saw her casually toss the mask on the fire. Other witches howled in excitement and crowded in.

Another witch came forward, the one whose mask was horned like the devil. He also took off his mask and behind it there was no face at all, but only the black, booming darkness of infinite space. He too burned the mask and danced. We all did. I was the light as air thing, the will-o-wisp thing, but also the great conjoined beast. I danced back and forth between those polarities. I danced the ecstasy of the Sabbat and danced with the Fire itself.

Moon 11

Building the Community of Souls

Our deep minds have learnt which sensory information seems important to our conscious mind and supplies it vividly. It is no coincidence that the average Marxist lives in a horrid world full of class struggle ... or the average magician in a reality full of gestures, signs, omens, power zones and etheric radiation. We teach our deep minds which experiences are important to us and ought to be emphasized. This worldview very easily becomes habit and is rarely questioned as it seems utterly real and convincing. Before long we may forget that what we experience is not all that can be experienced, that we live in a selection, not in the fullness of all possible realities. When we remember that we select our reality we may remember to select a reality worth living in. (Jan Fries, *Visual Magick*)

The first and most obvious thing that is required for community is more than one person. Immediately we are talking about the negotiating of an imagined dividing line, we're talking about navigating an inter-subjective experience, where two or more people negotiate the terms for reality construction between them. We begin to think in terms structured for us by mainstream thinking: us/them, me/you, your best interests and desires versus my best interest and desires ...

But in truth if we are about to attempt true magical community we are at a crossroads where such boxed in conceptions of selfhood will soon unravel. As Bayo Akomolafe so eloquently describes this realm and its work:

> The indigenous wisdoms of the Yoruba people invite us to think of the world as a matter of crossroads. As an ongoing emergence of the manifold via surprising intersections and 'intra-actions'. When offering a prayer or a libation, the word 'asé' is usually spoken out loud in a call-response encounter – a word which many interpret as the Christian 'amen', but which goes further than just ending a sentence or indicating acquiescence to a sentiment. Asé is the music of the crossroads and the brokenness of all things. The concept of self and identity, re-described in the queer philosophy of asé, cannot conceive of the 'other' as 'negativity, lack, [or] foreignness'; it repudiates the idea of identity as 'an impenetrable barrier between self and other [that is set up] in an attempt to establish and maintain its hegemony.' In other words, just as you find bands of darkness in light, and a heart of light in the blackest shadow, the self and the not-self are not separate, and difference – though real – is not fixed, but dynamic and co-emergent. The crossroads is not the place that lies ahead, a one-time occurrence. All roads are crossroads; every highway a junction of intra-sections. Matter-mind ... reality ... every 'thing' is already a quilt whose sewers, human and

> nonhuman, are scattered across space-time – every object a node in the cosmopolitical, material-discursive traffic of things crisscrossing, cross-hatching, crossing-out, bleeding-in each other. Crossroads help us appreciate our inter-being/intra-becoming and help us realise that something interesting is always happening at the boundaries and borders of things, and not just in their core or centre.

Or as it has been stated in Wiccan lore: 'ye may not be a witch alone.' Anyone who tries to tell you they practise magic alone has failed to grasp the poetics of the magical act. Nobody acts alone, whether we are separate in our immediate space from other human bodies or not. As Akomolafe says we are all of us cross-hatched with one another, bleeding into (or being bled into by) other lives at all times. Nothing, not our desire for independence, to our politics or dietary habits can change this fact, only tinker with the details.

Many of those beings that interpenetrate with our reality do not have human bodies. And before we begin to even consider how two or more human-bodied beings conduct magic together we need to have a sense of ourselves as already in magical community, as already part of a web of reciprocation. Establishing Right Relations with the beings already present in your practice will set a firm cornerstone for further relationships. In short, it is less than wise to try to enter into magical community with other humans if you are still establishing harmonious connections with spirits of your dead, of the land, and those humans with whom you share daily contact.

In the over-culture we've previously worked, to Step Out from the most important dividing line between a collective of selves and Others is always the line we draw between the living and the dead. What could be more natural than to pair living/dead as opposing opposites? The seen and the unseen? Or the human bodied and non-human-bodied?

What if we were capable of going beyond these dichotomies in some semi-final way, to truly, consciously partake of the crossroads of reality mentioned above? Those with the Sight may already see the world this way, but will have been engaged in a life-long battle to maintain that they are not insane and that how they view the world is legitimate. A person born Sighted doesn't get to decide whether they see things in this manner, but most of us do, most of us have the tools now to decide how seriously we take realities that can't be bought, sold or given value by mainstream thought.

If instead of privileging the possession of certain kinds of material form we gave higher standing to the ability to change and grow, we might begin to measure 'death' differently. Instead of deciding who is living and who is dead based on the obvious criteria we might consider whose consciousness is still fecund with potential, who can still change direction and re-configure. Then we would discover that some who walk around among us holding the status of the living, clothed in flesh, are actually already deceased. Some others who have a signed death certificate still manifest themselves in the lives of the living with great vitality and vigour and continue to affect the course of history, their thoughts defining the horizons and vanishing points of our own perspectives, for better or for worse. If we no longer see them because they are called 'dead', we remain unconscious of their influence and a ripe field for the reoccurrence that the tidal zone of the Underworld is so famous for.

The retreating and repeating tides of the Underworld seas can be a hell-scape for some, stuck in their loop of worst experience they are doomed to relive the core of what they believe about reality, which is often just a reflection of what they believe about themselves. Limited as we are by our core stories, even as living people, many of us have already found our way to subtle hell worlds where we move around in various stages of necrosis.

Luckily we know as a species we are all capable of changing

our perspectives in a manner that includes and takes account of Otherworldly community. We are capable of seeing the world through different lenses. We can infer this because so many human cultures have a story about a time long ago when the veil between the worlds, or between reality and the dreaming reality, was not so very wide as it is today. The mere fact that humans are so almost universally capable of imagining such a state without normative borders or boundaries, strongly suggests that it's not outside our collective human experience.

This collective includes the dead. If someone in the up-line can think like that it will never be entirely forgotten by the living. People are notoriously bad at trying to imagine something completely outside the frames of reference for their species, as we pass into the dream of this world certain conceptual limitations are part and parcel of incarnation. Even the most imaginative creations of the human mind are usually a variation or re-combination of variations from real life. Try to imagine a colour outside the spectrum we perceive with the human eye, or a creature not in some way made up of things Nature has already done. You will find we aren't too good with this.

The positive side of this limitation is at some level that we must have it within our potential to experience a world where the boundary between what is perceived as physical and imaginative experience (imaginal) phenomenon collapses. It does so disastrously in the lives of many schizophrenics, and creatively in the great mystical artists of history, but to some extent it remains a potential that, as some of us possess it, is latent in all.

When we talk about community many of us tend to abruptly stop thinking like occultists and slip directly into our own wounds. This is hardly surprising as the inter-personal zone is where all our hurts seem to emerge. Magic offers for many an illusion of escape from the inter-personal, to retreat into a world purely of their own creation, about them and their own empowerment. So it's common to hear very mundane language used to discuss working with others, as though we suddenly don't have any of our tools, and all our armour and prior assumptions have just flown back into position!

People will talk about setting boundaries, power dynamics, trying to negotiate power, and many other issues that assume the eternal supremacy of relations based on power-over. Because our models are usually taken from governmental sized institutions we tend to be only able to think in terms of absolute monarchy, democracy or full consensus. We assume power-over to be the natural main question of all human groups at all times and that locking in a lot of procedures and formalities must guard against its ravages. Instead we would do well to look at how smaller groups, such as indigenous tribes and clans operate, from a large variety of different cultures and consider some things outside the box rather than these central fixations. If we go into this thinking about how we are going to stop each other becoming fascist dictators we are obviously not going into this either with people we feel the right way about, or perhaps instead, when we fixate on power-over, it is ourselves we are worried about?

We see our own cultural preoccupations (hundreds of years in the building) writ large over the nature of every other people that has walked this earth, expunging their differences between groups in an act of mental colonisation that is mostly unconscious and deeply insidious. We even engage in this kind of unconscious projection when we try to imagine the lives of other species of hominid whose culture we know next to nothing about, and yet make endless assumptions about. We assign alpha/beta ideas to wolves that may have a totally different idea about what holds their families together.

What if instead of looking the Medusa directly in the face we worked to establish a space for something other to emerge without knowing its exact shape but allowing it to blossom forth from the magic of connection? What if the first and most important factor was where those humans stand with the dead and the land they're standing on and the health of all else that hangs upon it? Rather than foregrounding our human political machinations if we removed ourselves from the centre stage of things? What if there is no such thing as power-over another being that didn't include one's own oppression? What if there is no thing which is truly Other to your experience of life? How would you and a group of others treat each other if you were rooted in the Crossroads, if it were impossible for you to forget your interconnection?

It's probably hard to imagine, like those colours you've never seen before, but that doesn't matter, one doesn't need to be able to see and control the end to begin to walk down the path. This is the job of the creative arts, or writing, poetry and music, to cross over the hedge and bring back something Other and make something we couldn't previously imagine visible. To give us a glimpse of ways of being we haven't imagined yet, and therefore give us options, open our eyes to ideas for destinies we haven't even thought to want yet.

Allowing the Otherworld and the land to be the centre of your community of souls, building around that, learning from the way collaboration and harmony is established in the different regions of the spirit world, studying the art of networking understood to the intelligences of the forest, these things can allow us a taste of new possibilities. This is why magic is the Art; it allows us to become injectors of potentials.

Self-conscious modernity seems to come hand-in-glove with a fading awareness even of recent history, and repetition of its loops. If you think of the human collective unconscious as being inside us, the microcosm, just as the Underworld is within the body of the earth, you will see how larger issues and smaller ones are not disconnected. If something is forgotten, repressed, unspoken or unresolved it will reoccur with tidal persistence until it is dealt with. It rests in the earth still when no human remembers it anymore.

Much of the issues we face as a society today seem to be repetitions of recent history and this is no accident. It is because we are not taking care of the dead, we are not satisfying their grievances, we are making them memorials outside in town squares instead of part of our lives, and so parts of our human world, a place supposedly for the living, are slipping into hell-worlds, acting out historical loops of conflicts that seem unbreakable. In the grip of these fate-loops (if people find the word 'hell' too confronting) we lose access to Other modes of being within the human realm, let alone those outside of it.

For this reason I want us to talk about alternative ways of experiencing connection that are not from our own time-starved, 'swipe left, swipe right, text back immediately with emoticons if you truly love me', culture. We need to hear stories about something, like the nineteenth-century art of Romantic friendship for instance, before we're likely to experience that emotion. How many people saw Anne of Greengables as a child and gifted a friend with a lock of hair as a result?

Of course some people are trailblazers and have all sorts of experiences and feelings with no name long before they had heard about something like it. Someone has to be the one to create new names for things, after all. It remains true for most of us still that once something has a name and a few stories are written about it more people begin to find that mode of being a 'feelable feeling'. This is why we have such fierce culture wars over what kinds of themes we are willing to depict in movies and TV. Once there are both words and stories about something it becomes increasingly feelable. People trying to control or censor creative content are trying to control far more than how we entertain ourselves.

When a new word is invented or a new tale told and something becomes feelable it moves from being conceptual, that is a feeling you can conceive of or understand the concept of but not know yourself, to something you are able to feel personally. The idea that having words to convey certain emotions makes them more prevalent has been backed up by studies in neuroscience, (which I will include in the bibliography along with the sources of any quotes I've used or other writers who have influenced me). What has been discovered in this area suggests we should engage language with a greater dynamism if we want to extend our emotional range, and not hesitate to create new words or variations on words where none exist.

This is important to communities because the wider the range of feelable scenarios and emotions a culture has the richer its interior life and the greater range of personalities it can tolerate within its structure. Tolerance for difference isn't just important for non-violence, it's important for humans to be functioning at their best, which in my view includes the ability to perceive the Crossroads where our lives as discreet beings meet and affect each other in countless ways. For want of this perspective we fight nearly every culture-war battle we've ever waged.

Groupings that draw from a very narrow set of narratives will struggle to hold much difference within their community. Holding difference doesn't mean repressing people's resistance to someone very different to them, shaming friction and telling people how they ought to feel. It involves more of a preemptive strike where having shared stories that can hold that level of difference and make it meaningful and coherent for people. Does your worldview or tradition have a way to make such friction fruitful, stories that work like the alchemist's flame to transform conflict interactions into intra-actions that aid the individual practitioner in their own development?

Stories, and their magically active counterparts – myths, should always remain the very opposite to dogmas. *They should open up new pathways of behaviour and experience rather than shutting avenues down with regulations.* For this reason the tales that hold together the glue of a community should be multiple, messy, jagged with variations that are held as equally valid, full of moral contradictions that force people out of the comfort zone of adherence and into the vital environment of creative reverie and discursive reality explorations. Whatever these stories are that hold your people together they will have to be strong enough and wyrd enough to side-step, evade and eventually yield-to-conquer the narrower stories that new people will bring with them into the group. Most magical communities overreach themselves with how much material from the over-culture they think they can transmute and end up having their fragile internal culture overrun with friction, rather than being able to transform that friction into the sand that in the tender body of the oyster creates the pearl.

When people attempt to foster magical communities they will enter with certain stories they believe about groups, almost certainly the assumption of the centrality of power-over in all human interactions will be their mental resting point. The concept of an intra-action will remain for some time just that, a concept. They will continue to either act out a power-over model, or be in reaction or rejection of some previous model they've experienced.

Coupled with a scarcity and competition mindset, a need for group validation and we have all the fuels necessary to create jealousy and possessiveness. People generally won't think about these lenses as a myth they subscribe to, a prior religion, but as self-evident truths, and like all core beliefs they will manifest in some way for the practitioner. For those not ready to go beyond their personal 'interaction myth' only a desert of impossible people will be found, individuals you just can't work with, people who have unfixable problems, people who just don't understand your magic or your super unique personality ... The responsibility for fixing this pattern is given to mankind and taken away from self. It is the other people's fault, this person seems to say, things are just like this and so I walk alone.

When these toxins express in the manifest world and have their natural way with a group, bitterness ensues and one needn't cast a pebble in any direction very far to hear the tales of disappointment with coven life, or orders people have joined, or this or that abusive guru-figure. People come to the conclusion that groups don't work, people are bad, or that alternatively there is something uniquely not group friendly about their own personal disposition. In other words, their experience is either their own fault (possibly in a way that glorifies their charmingly acerbic curmudgeonly ways) or it is the fault of congregating with other magical practitioners in general.

What if the problem is the premise, the questions we start off with, that are leading us to conclusions and answers that seem to be very repetitive? When so many tell almost exactly the same story, just with different protagonists, it is a sure sign that the air up here is too thin, (with story-upon-story stacked upon each other, the free market stacked on top of empire, stacked on top of industry, teetering away precariously) that for all the claims of occultists to be Other we very seldom manage to bring back into the world of man anything other than the same old conclusions and mistakes. And those who are managing rarely speak of their successes, and if they do they aren't half as loud as the negatives. When repetition comes along, it's clear we've wandered into one of those fate-loops we mentioned and there is no personal-power to be had inside one of those.

To remedy this, or instead perhaps to enrich the soil from which other possibilities can grow, let's look in unlikely places, in the world of the dead and that other country connected to theirs by submerged archipelagoes, the past. To contact both of those places, and begin to move towards a new kind of community of souls, we are going to need to start by slowing down. This won't be easy because everything in our world rewards speed. It rewards busyness and the appearance of continuous work. But the work we need most requires an activity that is the mother of all creativity: *dynamic reverie.*

Once again, it might seem strange to begin a chapter about building community and then talk about the lonely art of solitude and deep thought. Please bear with me though, because one cannot begin to lay places for the two most important relationships you will ever experience if you have none of your own thoughts or self-knowledge to bring to the table. The art of friendship begins inside ourselves and getting ourselves to the place where we are ready to meet another person, not just in the casual, rushed, mutual trade of complaint and encouragement common way, but as *an art.*

We seldom think enough of the friendship we form with our first other magical practitioner and first important spirit/god, and how the qualities of those two formative connections will determine so much about the culture that will form up around you. If you are only just getting started you have the privilege of being able to entertain mindfulness right from the start.

Entering an already set-up group will be a different matter. I have mentioned what to look for in previous chapters and what to avoid, but here I will add a little. Rather than trying to enter the culture of a group as a whole it is often better to enter via friendship with one person in particular. A deep friendship of the type I am about to discuss. From that solid foundation I would attempt to next get to know the person in this new community with whom your friend is most closely bonded. This will give you a better idea of the culture of the group than simply knowing your friend, if you only see it through their eyes you will get a partial view. Bonding with your friend's-friend consciously will allow you to gain experience in navigating a three-way, magically active, friendship. You will benefit from that before you make a serious effort to bond with everyone in a group of five or more.

Whilst I suggest you need to begin with this kind of solidification, do try and find out as much about what the other people in this community are like as you can. Who does your friend identify as least like them and why? These kinds of questions will tell you a lot about what kind of diversity of personal characteristics the group tolerates (or even hopefully celebrates), and will bring up questions for you about how wide your own tolerance for difference extends? What stories does the group tell about the utility of difference and 'growth-friction'?

Romantic friendship is a platonic, but intense devotion and often artistic connection between people. The concept evolved in the nineteenth century under the influence of another new word 'sensibility', a glorification of sensitivity and emotional depth that attempted to balance out the Enlightenment's preoccupation with reason and logic. This kind of friendship often includes acts of devotion such as the wearing of each other's hair in lockets, keeping of tender mementos and tender reunions that would normally be reserved in our age for those with whom we have, or hope to have, a sexual connection.

So connected is romance and indications of high positive regard with sex in the over-culture that we even have the term 'friend zone' which frames anything not resulting in genital contact as a kind of cruel trickery where feelings are extracted without sexual payment rendered! This is a story that tells us something quite opposite to what Romantic friendship espoused. It tells us that other people are commodities, resources, investments that are either paying off or faulty. People just don't have time, you see, why should they waste the small amount of hours given to non-busy-ness on something that doesn't appease their most obvious appetites? When the soul is hungry the body seeks its own kind of comfort food. This being said, the best kind of sexual connections are usually those which evolve out of passionate friendship, so we do our sexual selves a disservice with this lack of patience, this lack of enjoyment of journey ...

I say that Romantic friendship (capitalized on the *R* to indicated I mean the era of the early nineteenth century termed the Romantic Age, as opposed to small *r* romantic as in 'romance novel') often involved artistic elements, but in fact it is closer to an art form itself. The poet Novalis and his circle coined the term: *symphilosophising*, to express the kind of conversation about deep matters driven not by one person's thought-contribution alone, but by many minds playing together in a verbal symphony.

This is the way our stories need to play together to practise fruitful magic together. You need to be able to experiment with this with at least one person on each side of the Veil, before it will be possible to properly imagine a healthy, co-operative group of this sort. It doesn't usually just drop into your lap, and most of the people I hear decrying how groups don't work have gone at trying to establish one in a totally inorganic way which exhibited little patience for the need for a fathom's deep formative friendship, or two, at the centre.

So, other than keeping bits of one another's hair, (a strongly charged sort of behaviour for a magical practitioner as hair is a traditional object link!) how can we actively foster a different story about friendship in our lives? I plan to give you an activity to do for this moon that will address this practically, head on. But first I'd like you to listen to a testimonial about friendship from an old-school gentleman whom I consider to be one of the most skilled people I know when it comes to establishing friendship and harmony with others.

> I've always been fascinated by other people and their stories. Especially the secret ones that aren't easy to get at. Even as a child I used to stare in through nighttime windows and wonder how the secret life of the people inside differed from the face they showed in the street. I never minded the difficult personalities either, the people who were what we might politely term taxing. Idiosyncrasies and so-called deformities interest me.
>
> When I met my best friend I recognized we were kindred

spirits, and also that we were very different in some ways. I occupied space in a very sensually comfortable manner, and he was often referred to by adults as 'away with the fairies'. It was, and is still today, every bit as much those differences I enjoy as the parts where we share an easy symmetry. It never occurred to me until other people put the idea there later that someone else liking to do a task differently, or enjoying different things to myself, was a negative. Difference was a pleasing anomaly before I was taught others found it an irritant.

So I would ask too many questions, saying all the time: why do you like to tie them or fold them like that particularly? I suppose I was a very friendly sort of pedant! I wanted to know why they did that thing in that manner and what it meant to them and I was prepared to follow people home sometimes to find out. (That was in the days before the word stalking became synonymous with everything dark and threatening.) Not because I had romantic designs on them mind you, but driven by a kind of interpersonal curiosity about their lives.

Friendship meant I'd convinced them to let me into their house for a closer look at their doings! I myself was a precise boy when it came to standard of execution and attention to detail, but I could also be rambunctious and full of energy, which led me to be scolded for getting my clothing dirty. For me everything was wound up tight for the joy of its big unravel, every carefully pressed and buttoned outfit, every crisp folded sheet was there to be disheveled when its time came. That process of closing and opening things and people is of great interest to me.

I think people who are good with people are sort of more aware of their own suppressed elements and maybe less judgemental of them. That loose rangy puppy part of me that wanted to get out and run around and lick people wanted a friend with a looser grip on physicality to take me spinning into the sky. In that friendship I discovered someone similar who, instead of mocking me for my anal retention had a part of him that wanted to become more controlled and precise and to inhabit space with more of the same gravity I did. It was as though I stuck my friend to earth a little and he lifted me up, or perhaps we took turns. He said my keen ear improved his music. This is how it is with all truly creative friendships, there's an exchange process, which is triggered by love. Not romantic love necessarily. I mean the love of something different for the sake of itself, the realisation that something can be lovely for itself only without it serving you in some way, without it being put there for me or my comfort, or directly answering my desires. Most relationships are wasting away for this kind of spaciousness.

What I call Love starts from that ability to celebrate both sameness and complementary opposition in a relationship, and if there is a final god of gods, then to me that God is Love. So many look only for sameness and wonder why neither their relationships nor friendships maintain any spark and their personalities collapse into one another. And don't think that friendships don't need spark just like a romance! Once you lose that vital alchemy where there's some kind of chemical reaction going off between the two of you as intellects, and as emotional beings, a friendship can die off as easily as a romance if it's not tended. To be vital friendships need some breathing space, some time without contact, a space to have time to read and experience and grow and bring back those riches to each other so you both make a unique contribution to the relationship. Solitude is as important to your friendship as companionship.

There should be a right mixture of mystery and relaxation also. You should at once feel comfortable enough to wear your nightclothes around them but also be inclined to put something nice on when you know you were meeting up for a special outing just because it fills you with a sense of occasion. Your friend is the one who you keep your best for, but also the one who knows what you look like when you messy cry.

They used to call it 'Romantic friendship' back before everyone started to worry so much that it might sound homosexual. I think it would be nice if it could exist with the opposite sex also, though perhaps I'd have not been so good at that as a younger man ... There is so much talk these days about the friend-zone, as though friendship were this lesser thing that should be equated little value, almost a form of insult! I retain the memory of a young male sex drive and so naturally I understand why young males want to move from this zone into other higher contact forms of intimacy. What I've learned though is that everything of value starts off from inside what they call the friend-zone. If you want a relationship with that woman you're lusting after you better consider what kind of friend she'd make otherwise you have much misery ahead for both of you.

That's where your real connections with all people start. If you don't have someone in your life, at least one person, that you could tell anything, that you know would rush to your aid through any adversity, for whom you save the best of yourself, with whom you enter into a non-critical but highly improving relationship where you both challenge each other at times also, with a kindly firmness when they know you are being less than you truly are, you need to find such a person. It's more important even than physical love. If you can find both together that is a sublime thing, but if I were asked to choose only one, and having known them both in their separate forms, I would always choose friendship.

In a magical friendship there is even more reason to aim high when it comes to quality. Two practitioners working in harmony who truly have each other's back in life and in the Work are so much more formidable than six occultists at odds with each other who all push and pull in different directions. It takes time to build such friendships, ones that are truly rock solid even when a storm hits. We are seldom lucky enough that they spring out of the ground fully formed. So it is probably fair to say that one of the leading reasons why occult groups so often fail the test of time, or provide less than pleasing results, is rushing.

Nonetheless, there are some practices that we can do to move in the direction of having a connection of this type. It is worth spending far more than one moon on this, as this person will become, in time, so close to the centre of all your efforts as a practitioner of magic that the quality of that bond could make or break you. Here are some things to consider and work on over this month.

1. What were your early experiences of friendship like? Are there ways in which you can see these early patterns repeating later in life? These might sound like simple questions but it is amazing how much they often uncover about the kinds of loops we might be unconsciously continuing to live out. If there is a clear pattern or repetition of certain themes in your life around relationship this is a clear warning sign to play close attention to this area.

I once knew a man who was very enamoured of Systems Theory (in a nutshell the belief that nothing has a single cause or origin point but comes to pass as the result of complex systems of interaction) who used to meet women on the Internet. He would go through a process of intense and passionate correspondence with them which would cool off a little as time went on but would nonetheless involve this distant woman becoming a large part of his life in some way, contributing towards his work and investing herself deeply in it. She would eventually want to meet him in the flesh. The story my friend told about his experience at the time was that these women would meet him in real life and lose interest in him because the mystery of distance romance could never be lived up to by a real man. The onus or origin of this reoccurring pattern was usually positioned as resting upon the shoulders of the woman in question, or sometimes in his most charitable moods, human nature in general. Any attempt on my behalf to draw attention to the contribution his own actions were having in this loop he was living and perpetuating encountered resistance. He would read it as a criticism. In reality though, drawing attention to the contribution someone makes to their own repetitious experiences needn't be framed in terms of blame, but in terms of desire for their liberation. It wasn't his doing alone either; something in him met something in the women who were looking to play out a complementary pattern they were stuck in. As Systems Theory would seem to suggest there was no single origin of the repetition.

Some New Age philosophies argue that you only get what you attract in life and this contains within it a rather privileged sort of assumption that can lead to victim-blaming. What were the Tasmanian Aboriginal people putting out there to the universe to attract invasion, conquest, and near extermination? On the other hand we should not fly to the opposite extreme of assuming the total opposite to be true. Abnegating all participation for things that just keep happening to us isn't an empowering road for the occultist, nor is Othering the perpetrator to the extent that you start seeing things in black and white.

There is, to be sure, a third way between those two extremes. I'm not asking you to see yourself as to blame for a whole chain of abuses or betrayals meted out to you by so-called friends, but neither am I asking you to simply give your power over to others by assuming you in no way can effect the things that happen to you. Your contribution might be innocent, such as a persistent naivety about the intentions of others, but it is important that whatever it is you bring it to light and select a different story for yourself going forward. Selecting it won't just make it magically drop out of the sky on you; you will have to work for it. This may not be as easy, but this is the occult and nobody said it would be.

2. Write down all the qualities that would be possessed by your perfect friend. Look over the list and consider if you yourself possess these same qualities? Are you looking for things in someone else you can't or don't intend to reciprocate? For instance, my Systems Theorist friend was looking for a Muse, someone that would show enthusiasm for his work in a kind of on-tap way, at this point in his life he was not interested in relationships based on mutual enthusiasm for each other's work. If non-mutuality is written into the terms of the agreement (for make no mistake, like any relationship a friendship of a magical nature possesses its own internal agreements, most of them made without either party being verbally explicit about the terms) even if you believe that your attention or thoughts are of higher value than theirs which is therefore its own sort of reciprocity, be assured the seeds of the relationship's eventual death are already present.

If you wonder why some pattern loops and keep happening to you, often you need look no further than this: generally one party wants something out of the other party that they consider their unspoken privilege to have without having to give the same in return. Perhaps they learned this as children, perhaps they just have strong appetites for certain things, such as attention, that they've never really had to check because when one person's patience ran out they could just find someone else? With the disposability of modern relationships where 'ghosting' (disappearing from all forms of contact without explanation) has become a common way for connections to end, it is often far easier to find another person to do it all over again with than it is to fix what went wrong with the first one.

3. Now ritually destroy the list that you made. That's right, you read that correctly, burn the list.
I have seen a lot of magic over the years that started with a list of qualities wanted in a lover or person followed by a spell to obtain a person like that. It's usually a very successful form of magic. The spirits like it when you get specific. When people get specific like that someone very often appears that fits the bill for the qualities wanted. The less positive aspect is that I've seldom, if ever, seen this kind of magic make two people happy … The problem seems to be that what we think we want and the relationships that would really lead to our best possible self-developing are two different things.

This happiness short-fall does not seem to be because one person's will has been manipulated with magic, (as there are multiple ways in which we all act on and affect and influence each other all the time, magic is just another one of those ways) the problem goes back to the premise of the magic. The premise, the opening statement of that kind of magic, is that friendship or relationship is about *what you hope to gain from it,* that it's about certain ways in which you expect to find someone with a personality that satisfies all the requirements you have. As if they are a means to an end. Nearly everyone starts from this premise and yet simultaneously hopes to be accepted, loved, appreciated and celebrated for the unique person they are!

True love, (and remember that I don't mean for this to exclude friendships or connections with spirits), does not get started because someone is presented to you to assuage your every longing and sit comfortably around all the structures and defence mechanisms you already have in place. Real love is about turning toward the person, people, or entities that always have your back and making a decision to love them with the same fierceness you believe you could have loved this perfect person … This is where the growth often is to be found, and the best fruit.

4. When you consider the above proposition, the fact that you may already have in your life so much more possible and available love than you currently choose to invite or accept, how does that make you feel? What kind of resistance do you experience to the idea? Because clearly you do possess resistance, otherwise you would already be reciprocating and enjoying.

Perhaps you find yourself thinking of when your current friend said a really wrong thing about a matter you're excruciatingly sensitive about? Or that one time you told them about the guy you had a crush on and she still flirted with him? Or maybe they always complain about not having enough or their life being hard when anyone can see that your life is indeed far harder and you have far less than them!

Now have a look back over the offences that have created armour between you and this person, and make those responses about what you felt rather than about what they said or do. Why does it bother you when they complain of this thing or do that thing? Is there a part of you that would like to complain also but has been biting its own tongue virtually since birth? When you've looked at each item on your list like that you might find you cross a few off as really not worth resenting your friend for.

Perhaps their success in a certain area or their charisma has always 'made you feel' incompetent? If your friend can make you feel then they will be stronger than you in this magical relationship, and that won't end up being good for you. Two closely matched people will work the best magic together. If you work through whatever their behaviour brought up for you, you may find that much of this armour that has built up as resistance to love between you and them is based on a collection of times when they didn't fulfil your every friendship desire. This infant inside us, this part of the self that looks out at the Other demanding it satisfy us, and conform to a certain shape in order to do so, needs to die off and be reintegrated to allow us to do adult magical relationships to the best of our ability.

Not expecting people to conform to our dream idea of a friend or lover is one thing, taking abuse or rampant non-reciprocation is another. We are trying to walk a third road here, a middle road between extremes. We do not want to declare that everything is our own fault, or our friend's. Ideally we will reach a place together where the question of fault is moot and there is only a mutual dross to be disposed of after the alchemical flame has been through us.

Every supposed fault of our partner's will become a tool in our sculpting. But they must be sculpted along with us, and so, if there are behaviours you just can't let go of even when considered in terms of what you yourself are bringing to the situation, you must discuss it with your friend. To just stone-wall or give the cold shoulder is a decision to allow the friendship to die rather than face the discomfort or discussion. Instead of accusing, try to consider they have better intentions than you have been assuming, try to imagine you are asking them to help you understand rather than telling them off. If they become defensive you may need to remind them that you aren't attacking or judging, you just want to understand why they do this thing because it's affecting you in some way.

It's important that both you and your friend know that shame won't assist either of you. Trying to shame or punish your friend is not the aim here, you aren't trying to get-even you're trying to understand how and why their perspective differs from your own as much as it does. When you become conscious of punishment behaviours in yourself you might be shocked to discover how often you as an adult set out to punish other adults for perceived failings in small and big ways. This isn't really your fault that you absorbed this pattern, as we live in a culture which is very punitive where using emotional forms of punishment was bred into us since childhood through every example.

If you do this properly, really attempting to imagine into their experience you will find it makes it easier to get into a circle and work magic with this person. All harboured resentments will become road-blocks of resistance to your future work together and can even escalate, if envy becomes a factor, into actual magical sabotage of evil-eye proportions. So this isn't just a feel good activity by any stretch of the imagination, as magic tends to grow whatever is present in a relationship. It is crucial that two or more people not go into an act of magic together with undiscussed issues between them, as magical work will amplify or bring to the surface with a big bang, whatever factors and conditions are already present.

It would be very helpful if the person you are working with can read this book. As happened to my Systems Theorist friend, even someone who knows the theory can fall prey to repetitions of pattern when it comes to their own self, especially once they are on the defensive and have hinged something of their selfhood on the need to 'win'. All of us, no matter how reasonable, are vulnerable to missing what we easily spot in another, if we can learn to take a helpful rather than a critical approach the person who is willing to constructively and supportively point out loops or patterns of behaviour in you that might be invisible to your own eyes becomes your greatest ally.

Failing (for now) a person in your life who does this, then, you are going to need to cultivate such a relationship with a spirit being. I am always suspicious of spirits (and people) that tell me everything I want to hear. Such a spirit is not your friend anymore than such a person is. Either insincerity is present, which means the entity has an agenda of some kind, or you are beginning to selectively hear! This can be particularly tempting for those who have a story about themselves that says they are a difficult person to get along with as they may struggle to hold onto human friendships. Making friends with spirits that never contradict any of your favourite assumptions and viewpoints might seem relaxing now, a refuge from the cruel world of man, but it won't help you develop stronger sorcerous practice or become a more empowered person.

A good spirit, like a good human companion, will risk annoying you when it becomes necessary to step between you and a self-destructive decision or major misstep or even to stand right back and let you fail when you need to. Never shoot the messenger or ignore messages that don't please you. When a spirit, or indeed a human companion to your work, approaches you with difficult matters always lead in by saying 'thank you for coming to me with this' or 'thank you for letting me know.' Treat both roles with a certain sanctimony, as if it were a privilege to be part of this other person's process of becoming, for it is.

5. Consider the stories that created and solidified your friendship. What is the story of your meeting? The main narratives you both love and use as frames of reference? What is the story that frames your friend's magical practice? Is there a tale of some sort, perhaps with mythic qualities, behind who they are as a magical being, what their backstory is in being here in this incarnation and what it is they are here to do? Most occultists, if pressed by someone they truly trust will reveal they've always known they had a mission of some kind. How does what they're here to do in the human world sit with what you're here to do? Are there ways you could both better uphold each other's mission? Do you know this already about your friend and they you or will you need to buy some wine and have a deep chat with them? Try to encourage an environment of mutual interest where there ceases to be their story and your story as two discreet things and an 'our story' is created.

Be wary of who is telling that story, make sure there are opportunities for both of you to be driving that inspired process forward, never fall into the trap of expecting special treatment based on an unspoken assumption of privilege in the relationship. If you want to lay the foundations for a truly enduring partnership around which a group of practitioners may eventually form up then it is in your best interests to promote this reciprocity. Because if there is a lack of it in some way this foundation won't hold when you try to build on it, resentments will undermine it. I have learned this the hard way on both sides of that power imbalance, and whilst such arrangements may even last a long time they will not last ultimately.

6. If your friend is willing you might ritualize the beginning of your journey as working partners by sitting comfortably together in the circle and engaging in extended eye contact. While you gaze into your friend's eyes what do you feel? Is the intimacy uncomfortable? Is it hard not to crack up? Why do you think you find this uncomfortable or want to step aside from the closeness of it via humour? Consider and lean into all these feelings for the first five minutes.

For the second half of a ten-minute session I want you to gaze on your friend as a manifestation of their patron deity. If they do not have a soul god, or a patron, or a specific divinity they relate most to then you might have to pick an entity whose power most reminds you of a godly version of your friend. Imagine that every quirk and idiosyncrasy of their nature and their face is an expression of that divine force in some way. What is the deity trying to tell the world by appearing in your life in this manner? While you are doing this your friend should do the same with you, at the end you bow to each other or give a gesture of respect. Practise this as often as you can throughout the moon cycle.

7. Share what I call your 'parent texts' with one another, the books and films that have shaped you in some way, and ask your friend to do similar with you. Enquire and discuss the story behind the story, the reason why this particular movie or book is a window into the psyche of your friend. This interest you

are taking in another person might seem like work to some of you and may not come naturally, but remind yourself that this energy will come back to you in the form of a more powerful magical connection with someone. And when it comes to magic, the pack (if built correctly on blood-brotherhood and deep loyalty) is always harder to defeat than the lone wolf witch.

Moon 12

How to Go in Among Them

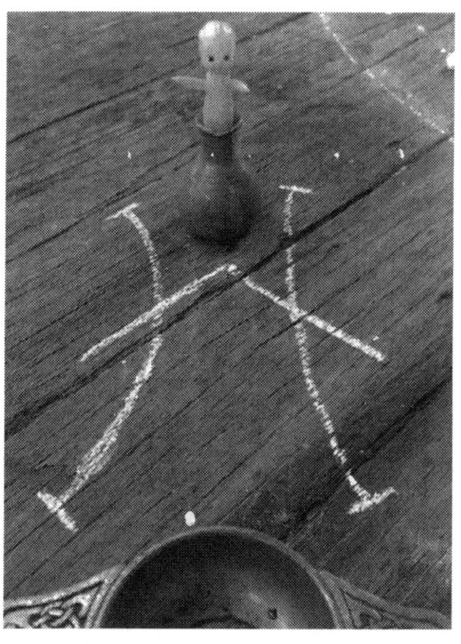

Be silent and listen: have you recognized your madness and do you admit it? Have you noticed that all your foundations are completely mired in madness? Do you not want to recognize your madness and welcome it in a friendly manner? You wanted to accept everything. So accept madness too. Let the light of your madness shine, and it will suddenly dawn on you. Madness is not to be despised and not to be feared, but instead you should give it life ... If you want to find paths, you should also not spurn madness, since it makes up such a great part of your nature ... Be glad that you can recognize it, for you will thus avoid becoming its victim. Madness is a special form of the spirit and clings to all teachings and philosophies, but even more to daily life, since life itself is full of craziness and at bottom utterly illogical. Man strives

> toward reason only so that he can make rules for himself. Life itself has no rules. That is its mystery and its unknown law. What you call knowledge is an attempt to impose something comprehensible on life.
> (Carl Gustav Jung)

One of the consequences of having left the bundle and doing the work of these thirteen lunar cycles is the horrifying recognition of the true extent of the madness of human society, or even of human life itself. Perhaps you thought you already saw it and are now appreciating how deeply that madness had made ingress. People new to this perspective often have the initial response to pull away, to condemn, or to attempt to purge one's life of people who still seem trapped in its thought-matrix. In fact, if you're just starting out on the path of magic and these twelve moons have been your first as a budding occultist you are quite likely to find yourself at this stage around this very time. In my tradition we refer in casual terms to this as the one-year blues. So be wary of pursuing anything too extreme in regards to action at this time.

It's usually best not to act too impulsively at this time but to observe the feeling rising and falling and allow the feeling to blossom and mature before acting out of it. Impulsive moments of following your gut certainly have their place, but you need to be careful of purging people from your life when you are really just afraid of being pulled back into similar behaviours yourself. Is it really them making you feel so bad? Or is it the way their loops threaten to pull you back in to your own previous patterns?

It is quite possible it's not being around that 'muggle' who doesn't get it that's the problem, but the internal doubts about your own obtainments the person's presence brings out in you. This will be especially strong if that person happens to be a parent or a lover. If you act now from that place of insecurity, trying to make yourself secure by surrounding yourself only with people who entirely conform to your worldview, you will regret it later when you have obtained the quiet strength that no longer requires social approval. The quiet strength that does not shrink from things Other to its own nature but inspects them with curiosity.

It is best, once again, to avoid looking the Medusa directly in the face. Instead of using up your energy railing against all those who don't understand the new wonders opening before you via magic, pour your mental and emotional resources into building those rich connections we've laid the groundwork for in previous chapters. As tempting as it would be to take it one step further and *only* focus on such relationships, it is highly unlikely that your life allows you to do this.

For most of us there are jobs, extended family, even immediate family and friends who do not practise who will continue to be part of our life even though the you they once knew has been sacrificed, died, decomposed and been entirely reconfigured right under their noses. It may even feel deceitful how much you've changed and probably subsequently act when in their presence. But these acting skills are ones you will continue to need throughout your life, so it is best not to be too keen to abandon them.

Rudolph Steiner in his *How to Know Higher Worlds* talks about how a properly balanced occultist should not be made dysfunctional by their practice, but instead more functional. He defends this in the teeth of the assumption that all people interested magic are impractical and irrational individuals, so it is arguable it answers a false accusation. Yet I believe there is wisdom in his stance regardless, not only for the obvious fact that it allows us to thrive in our daily lives but because functionality draws less attention from the eye of the world.

To make going back into the world, whose values we've chosen to shrug off, a little more bearable and allow us to capitalize on our skills rather than become their victim, I have organised this moon around arranging our outer lives with the same intent and strategic thinking we should apply to our magic. We will organise the people in our lives inside one of three concentric circles with those we are magically intimate with in the inner circle, regardless of whether or not they are human persons. The next circle out will be reserved for those with whom you can be somewhat you but cannot share all aspects of your spiritual practice with them, and the third for those who must be seen entirely as needing to be 'managed'.

Before you sit down with a piece of paper to answer the question of whose names should go where, I'd like us to consider the activity from a philosophical angle. It's important to be conscious of what sorts of attitudes we hold about our fellow man as our expectations tend to bound in what we can experience. In other words, the frame we place on the real will become real for us. I've seen people meet someone whose existence they wouldn't have deemed possible in this world until they changed their sense of what was possible.

I've also seen this go a variety of unpleasant ways when people were locked into negative ideas about their fellow man. One of those happens when people still in the reactive stage, (where they fear being pulled back into their loops if they interact with people who share those same habit-traps), form their own groups. People like this tend to fill their coven's head with the idea that the world is a perilous environment full of people carrying parasitic attachments that could jump onto you and cause possession at any given moment, and you may be in danger if you go to visit your folks! I've seen this used to distance people from their families, a kind of isolating behaviour that is a warning sign of cult formation.

That kind of attitude can very quickly lead to mentalities where lodges or covens start to encourage the initiate to break away from all contact with families and old friends who don't practise or believe as they do. The kind of 'stepping out' this book advocates is not of that sort, it is a feat of consciousness that does not require total isolation from the general herd to uphold itself. Nor does the well-maintained occultist need fear parasitic intrusions simply from being in the company of the uninitiated! No great power should ever be so fragile ... Teaching people to be fearful and see their magical defences as so fragile is a magical health risk in itself.

Another misguided angle is to speak of the uninitiated in terms of being a lesser species. As tempting as this perspective can seem at times there are many great individuals among the arts, sciences and philanthropic communities who would never class themselves as mystics or sorcerers and yet in many senses See as clearly as some occultists.

Others among their number will behave so ignorantly that there will come times when you need to fall back on the old 'wolves care not for the opinions of sheep' homily. It is possible to come to a balance here, if one stretches the boundaries of either/or thinking as our practice inevitably will. The uninitiated are at once part of a single red beast of the blood with all living, a wholeness of which there is no Other, and at the same time, on a white instead of red level, think and see very differently to us.

Both these realities matter, and one will matter more than the other in some contexts and visa-versa in others. Our minds require this kind of flexibility to excel in the Work. We must not be pulled into the fruitless desert of their perspective because the way they see us is not uplifting or empowering to us, and we must not yield to agreeing with them. Yet we must not fall into supremacy thinking either, assuming ourselves separate in some ultimate way. For there to be a witch there must be a non-witch human being and most of us are born from parents who did not practise, or will ourselves produce children who don't. It may be argued the occultist is a flower upon the tree of humanity, but a flower cannot exist without the plant it grows on.

For the reasons mentioned above when we say managed we

mean no disrespect necessarily, only that there can be no deep mutual understanding between the two of you, and interactions that reveal this fact are likely to be upsetting for the uninitiated person. Place those in your outer circle whom you know you must entirely act around and cannot show your true self to.

Some people will try to say they have no such people in their lives but in truth this would apply to hardly any practising occultist. The world 'occult' means hidden for a reason and it is not appropriate to share every aspect of it with everyone. Anyone who went into this practice thinking it desirable to exhibit that level of openness will be in for a rude awakening if he or she tries to deal with the realm of faerie, or any magical practice which is stringent about secrecy and remaining non-verbal about what you have seen or been told.

Those who are in the outer circle are those you will probably want to interact with the least. It is tiring to keep up an act, so it's likely you will become moderately reclusive, but not pathologically so. Think of what you have in common with each of the people in the outer circle. There must be some reason why you have chosen not to cut them out of your life. What is that reason? If you can find a mask to wear with that person that focuses on your mutual area of interest you should be able to encourage them down predictable alleyways of conversation, which will not be stimulating to you but will allow you to maintain the illusion that everything is normal. Find ways that you can draw energy from this relationship in some way, rather than allowing them to just hook onto you, as is the common pattern in relationships between initiated and uninitiated folks.

Before we speak of the middle circle I'd like to reflect a little on the way that I'm using the word initiated. I don't mean this in terms of initiation into a particular magical fraternity or coven. Just as a nice way of referring to those who have dissolved, sacrificed and reconfigured their ego and social identity, thoroughly stepped outside of the dream of society and seen its constructs for what they are, and those who have not. Those who have and those who have not can never meet in any deep psychological sense, but may share physical needs with one another which can still be of fetch-driven profundity.

The middle circle is perhaps the most difficult to manage and is also highly important. This is the space in your life you make for the people who have a chance of one day being invited into your inner circle. At this stage you are still testing their depth and finding out if it can answer yours, or hold the things you would share, and if you yourself are willing to make a deeper space in your psyche and your life for shared story with this person. Or whether instead you wish to enjoy this interaction for what it is without striving for anything more?

Unless you've quite literally grown up with someone it generally takes a long time to develop real magical intimacy before you can attempt to work well with them. You don't want to rush that stage so it helps to have some sort of clearinghouse in your life occupied by people you really like to some degree. These people may never truly understand you but you aren't just physically dependent on them, or connected at the fetch, you are interested in their mind and feel some degree of spiritual or emotional affinity with them.

The central circle is for your blood-brothers and sisters, your magical working partners, you beloveds, the spirit beings with whom you share the deepest kind of trust and reciprocity. These people know your soul story, and you theirs, those stories are intertwined and it is impossible to imagine your own well-being without it being tied to theirs in some way. Part of who you are is invested in these people. It is with them you will be your most powerful as a sorcerer because these people believe in you utterly, but they will also bring out your ego and your wounds more than anyone else, because it is their good opinion that you are likely to want most. Because of both the glory and the pain of such connections, these souls will be the most effective transformative agents in your life.

Over this moon you will work on becoming skilled at entering the world inside the hedge without losing your edge. The devil-as-fate will continue to try to challenge you for your toad bone and in this metaphor the world and the devil are one and the same. Just as when Taliesin drank from the cauldron of Ceridwen, the witch was immediately alerted, causing Taliesin to need to display his new skills and show his worthiness to hold what he'd taken, the powers that be respond to strength with tests. The world will not make it easy for you to enter with your Otherness intact, but if you were opposed by anything less than the entire world it wouldn't be fair, after all, because you're a sorcerer.

You will need to get strategic about your Cloaking. Before you go into social situations where you will be exposed to the general public contract your cloak in tightly. Remember that your cloak isn't just a barrier it is an active egregore that turns poisons into nutriment. Look through your cloak after an encounter, denature and incorporate the energy from any negative materials that have adhered to you.

This will be the realm of madness in many ways, but if you can stop resisting it, you would have known madness to some degree in the process of noticing and working through what you yourself bring to the insanity of your previous relationships. It is only your judgement that things ought be some other way that makes madness so hard to deal with. See it as a challenge rather than a hardship, a test of your potential for adepthood. The less Fate is met with complaint and more with strategy the more stealthily it seems we sneak past the guard on the door that holds the elixir, the philosopher's stone, the toad's bone, the mead of inspiration ...

When you are amongst the crowd from your middle circle allow the Cloak to expand a little wider, creating an intelligent mist by opening its fibres wider. Use the warmth you feel towards these people whose company you enjoy to expand your red serpent energy and warm the threads of the black cloak, helping them to expand into fluffy fullness. Mentally programme the mist of your cloak to allow through the vision of you this person is ready to receive. Trust in the cloak to conceal what they are not yet ready for.

When you are with the people of your inner circle expand your Cloaks together, lightening them to gossamer thinness and allowing them to pass through each other's. Have each person open them wide until all are holding a wall of cloaks behind each other and forming a circle with them. All participants are holding a warding circle between their fellows and the outside world, this action says: I have your back.

But even more importantly, you are open to those inside without defence and observing each other magically without boundaries or evasion. Afterwards, all should re-fabricate their Cloak and push from the inside out any debris that might have landed there, denaturing it and including it in their Cloak. This way we prevent negative entanglements or dross being passed between people in a group, but at the same time we can grow from brief exposure to each other's toxins as well as powers. In the manner that inoculation can produce immunity so can this exposure empower our Cloak.

Throughout this moon find as many circumstances where you can practise these three conditions of the Cloak as possible. Regularly work on flushing your red serpent from the inside and adding debris to your Cloak, even after very pleasurable experiences. No matter how much you love the person you picked up the black fragments from they will do you better as part of your Cloak than they will wedged in your internal organs.

Moon 13

Rinse and Repeat

> I was walking in Shadow, seeking a place, a very special place. It had been destroyed once, but I had the power to recreate it, for Amber casts an infinity of Shadows. A child of Amber may walk among them, and such was my heritage. You may call them parallel worlds if you wish, alternate universes if you care to. I call them shadows, as do all who possess the power to walk among them. We select a possibility and we walk until we reach it. So in a sense, we create it …
> (Roger Zelazny, *The Guns of Avalon*)

Although this book is aimed at any practitioner or future practitioner of magic, it is written from a witchcraft perspective, as the author is himself a witch. I don't believe that fact makes it any less applicable to other traditions or paths, in fact I think it is key to the unexpected quality of some of the angles these exercises come at you from. There is something of the nature of the wild about true witchcraft, an edge of discomfort that is always radical and stretching, even to radicals, and occupies a kind of Other space which can never be wholly defined or confined in a single view derived from human politics. Its perspective is that of the wilderness, of the stars and wastes.

All the major human religions are based on a predicate that some states of existence are superior to others and must be transcended, controlled, punished or rewarded. Whilst from the perspective of the wilds beyond the hedge there are no parts of Wholeness that are less valuable than others, there is only what Buddhism would call skillful means, and we might call the cunning art of how to deal with each of them in the way most beneficial to ourselves and our communities.

So when we come across madness, either in the body of mankind as a whole, or in ourselves, we are merely looking at another potential tool, an aspect of our shattered potential that needs rebuilding, our always-already-realised-not realised, Wholeness. It may sound irrational, but if we are to swim in the current of madness and make of it divine madness, we mustn't stand-toe-to-toe to fight the madness of our society we must become skillful thieves and alchemists who loot from the crumbling effigies anything we think worth grifting, preserving, transforming or skimming the cream from. Our mental world as well as our physical world should begin to be based on metaphors of recycling, up-cycling and repurposing. In this way our spiritual approaches can be in better harmony with the behaviours our descendant will have to engage with to continue with what they inherit from us, and will make our leading metaphors relevant to the future. Any smart occultist is planning in advance how to be a useful ancestor and have people feed their memory.

This is why witchcraft may appear antinomian and of the left-hand path when in all honesty it both is, and isn't. Certainly, yes, the face of Wholeness that must consume the initiate is that of the most reviled and Othered of all the realms, the Underworld but even that dissolution medium is not Wholeness alone. Many don't get much further than this and come to the conclusion that Traditional Witchcraft is all about darkness and skulls, but this consists of a partial understanding only. The energies of darkness, death, decay, sex, taboo, wrath, pleasure, pain, dominance, submission and regeneration are all connected. Whilst they have their root to the world of death they feed the roots of the Tree of Life. Without this black serpentine monster of the Underworld gorging and disgorging its stomach, bowels and womb in multifarious creations and destructions, the earth body would be inert and without potency and yet so many humans story this force as evil and full of hell. It is we who have made it, through the shape of our interactions with it, into a hell realm.

The black serpent power is simply hungry. It can become blood hungry when it's ignored long enough … One doesn't really want to be stuck in the hell-loops that many people are knotted into, but that is hardly a sign, the mere fact that humans don't like it, that such forces don't play a necessary part in the universe. Our human-centric loathing for darkness and death leads to a great many of our mental problems as a species. For this darkness is also inside us, it is the darkness of potential that seeds need to thrive and open, that roots need to nest in, that bodies need to rot in and give their nitrogen to the dance of life.

The spirits that writhe and turn within the various hell mouths and vulvas of the Earth and inside her, rising up from bogs, grave-fogs and sea mists can be called 'spirits black'. They are the ones who stripped you bare of your preconceptions when you crossed the hedge, without them you'd still be carrying necrotic tissue of dead ideas. Nothing gets cleared away without their carrion-pecking beaks and sharp claws sloughing the flesh back. You can't be a creature that belongs only to the light and still carry much in the way of complexity. Every depth creates a darkness and in denying it with every street light, with every religious fixation on light, our species has woken a darkness beyond our own comprehension that rises to balance that neon-hued light we've held up as God or Reason.

If you feel there is still baggage you carry that belongs in your bundle but won't come off, it may be to do with your feelings towards this realm. Nearly every trope in every horror movie you've ever seen attempts to push buttons that stem from revulsion felt for the blackness, even racism is linked into this fundamental connection between 'light=good, dark=bad'.

You might need to find yourself meditating on decay like left-hand-path tantrikas before you try again to leave your bundle properly. Get as close to human remains as you are able until you find the edge of your discomfort and lean over it a little further. How does it feel to lie down atop a fresh grave? What about next to a dead person? Our society has made this difficult for you to experience, almost as if through some unconscious knowledge it senses the need to keep your own profundity from you. For as Lord Byron wrote 'life's profundity is in the grave'.

Without having felt the moment of vertigo in the presence of the corpse, as though the room is tilting away while all the dead one's memories are spilling like a torrent into the collective sea of old tears, how can we fully grow up? Their blood is joining the ocean of tears the world is shedding every day and with it, running away down the little canals in the embalming table and down the drain to the Underworld, and with it who they were is joining the all of Life in Death, and Death in Life ... They are 'forgetting, and forgetting, and forgetting' to quote Dylan Thomas's *Under Milk Wood* and yet the Underworld is remembering everything and keeping the accounts. They are drinking the waters of Oblivion, but the black serpent of the earth body is drinking from their

Well of Memory and taking notes.

When you've found the holiness in that hair-raising feeling and gazed in neutrality on the feast the maggot makes of flesh you might want to try leaving your bundle again. This is the gift of the black serpent Realm of the Underworld. It is all about discomfort, nothing about it is an easy form of pleasure, always a slightly distressed, aroused/disturbed state. This is why the world's religions have all spoken out against this realm and taught us how to flee from it, because basically it's just not fun in the simple sense. Above all else do not allow other things to be nourished by you because that involves being on the bottom instead of the top! And whether it's the food chain or the sexual act we have become quite obsessed with this type of prioritization of top over bottom.

The white serpent realm of the Heavens to most is still heaven and the Underworld is still hell, but we mean something different by it. The white serpent gorges and disgorges in the sky also, but his progeny are winds and storms and rains. Storms in the realm of consciousness and wild storms in the world are not disconnected. This is the Holy Spirit that animates us with consciousness this moving air, this in-breathing and exhaling of water and energy across the storm-lashed sky. So the desire to go to heaven is a desire to leave the earth to be absorbed back into a state of 'pure consciousness'. I place this term in inverted commas because it's an impossible state for an embodied being to comprehend in any way, shape or form.

We as humans are the children of the black earth, animated by breath, literally inspired, or in-breathed by the spirit of wind. Our origin in the darkness and the dirt has been denigrated, as humanity has joined together in great numbers to spit in the face of its mother. But this fact does not mean witchcraft or magic of any stamp should be a reactionary cult in response to this, for we are something far more revolutionary than just a reaction against mankind's collective mistakes.

We people of the outside are a force that dissolves contradictions, or dances dynamically with and within them, we are not limited to a reaction or a resistance movement, though we could certainly be the power behind one if it benefitted us. We use the power created by our own discomfort to ride our own sorcerous will into manifestation, or to track a possibility for miles until it becomes a reality. For this reason of far-seeingness we may also have covenants with the beings some call angels. Not just the serpent powers of the Underworld, the wailers at the gate and the washers at the ford, the yell hounds and the massing shades of the dead, but with beings of light so extreme that they hold terror as much as exaltation.

There is no tame and comfortable aspect to Nature, neither in the sky nor below the ground. Yet each and all whether pretty or not contain beauty. The spirits that have been called angelic are stellar, planetary or of the upper atmosphere. That they have been given Hebrew names is neither one way or the other from the perspective of this sphere, so universal are these powers. This doesn't mean some traditions won't have highly specific names for these entities, but just that they gloss easily and seemingly willingly with the Hebraic names for angels and sometimes Saints.

The white realm is a heady experience and the modern world is drunk on it. There is something intoxicating to the point of potential madness, of the type that makes us see chimeras in the desert about this type of magic. The fact that our society has over emphasized everything to do with the whiteness does not mean we can solve our ills by a reactionary shift away from it and replace it entirely with Underworld observances. Although this is the typical response of humans who don't know the cunning, when confronted with pretty much any problem, it is by far and away not skillful means. It constitutes a glance at the Medusa who will in turn make this new move as stone and unrelenting as its opposite.

When one party is pushed down and another placed above harm is done to both. I am placing that in italics with the suggestion you read that twice over. To be placed above another being in some way is just as harmful and distorting to the psyche as being placed below, though the effects may not be as immediately obvious. It teaches a person to disconnect from his 'inferiors', to over-estimate her own potential and importance and to repress all the aspects of himself that are reminiscent of the inferiors. Whilst the anger this creates is usually turned outward against the oppressed group, it is often turned inward as well.

This is harm that must be healed and worked with, not simply rebalanced on one side to change the position of oppressor and oppressed. If we deny the harm done to the one placed above we take a step away from truly owning our own interconnectedness, and we are going to have to do that going forward if we can find paths to surviving as a species with all the other species that have not yet gone extinct. We need to tell new stories that are flexible enough to enable both our oneness and our diversity.

Just as with oppression in the human realm, by suppressing the blackness in ourselves and Nature and obsessing as a culture about the head-rush we get from whiteness we have harmed our understanding of the white realm just as catastrophically as we've got ourselves out of Right Relations with the Underworld. We are well 'into the red' with our debt to the Underworld, but we've also insulted the powers above by deeming them antagonistic to that which is below. It is only inside ourselves that this antagonism is reified, where consciousness has become antagonistic to form. Recognising inside ourselves this anthropocentric approach to which spirits we choose to revere (formed perhaps on our personal taste after certain experiences in the past) we are able to remove our emotional load from our perception of the spirit world and see more clearly.

With that in mind, let us think again about these coloured

serpents inside the human person. The presence of a strong black snake in someone will stir up the presence of the Red, for these two are very attracted to one another. This can be seen in people in the way the darker energies excite lust in the form of incubi and succubi. The link between death and sexuality is expressed poetically as the intertwining of two serpents that are forever disappearing into and out of each other in an ouroboros of themselves. Life is forever feeding on Death, and Death upon Life.

This same story of serpents can be seen reflected in the human brain. For the sake of this poetic analogy the stem brain which is the part necessary to maintain all our unconscious functions links us with the world of the dead, who dwell in the belly of the black serpent brain. On top of it and unable to exist without it is the limbic system of the brain which is responsible for our emotions, dreams and intuitions and many of our instincts; a semi-collective place from which the instinctual intelligence of the fetch emerges as a distinct form, a temporary individuality in a red serpent sea of togetherness. The red serpent and the spirits that belong to this sphere seek oneness between tribal units and predation upon entities outside that bond; both are forms of assimilation, whether erotically or via consumption.

Usually seen as the brain's crowning achievement, the frontal lobe or neo-cortex is the part of us responsible for our so-called higher functions. But if you've heard what I've been saying about the levelling nature of witchcraft you will know I'm about to tell you that no one part of the dynamic system of human consciousness is more holy or less holy than another. There is no uniquely important achievement being made here at the front of our brains, no linear narrative of human development from lesser to greater which makes this form of intelligence superior to that of a forest network. Only wholeness requires precedence, anything that forms a web, a tissue of stories, interconnecting with each other in thousands of ways and holding a multi-textured sanctity that stretches across many orders of being. Thus see the eyes of the Great Whore who some have known as Mystery who gazes upon the profanities that man has made in his own image and sees nothing but sanctity slightly out of alignment. It is hers, the rider of the red beast, to consume all and reject none.

The neo-cortex belongs to the white serpent of inspiration and speech but is no more crucial or evolved than the other powers and classifications of spirits. There is a green serpent whose belly is full of the dancing ranks of faerie as they spin the gossamer fabric of the green realm into being with their songs and stories. Every tree, every fruit, every entheogen is an expression of their unalienable sanctity of the body of this collective gnosis bringer, these genius beings that speak the language of chemistry rather than that of words. If the green one moves in the brains of humans at all he comes as a stranger, he moves as a green power from outside the edges of things, from over the hedge, he steals like the spirit of the woodlands itself, up in and through the cracks in all the walled and fenced places. Slowly he takes apart what has been turned to stone, that which has assumed the hubris of the eternal.

The red serpent of the limbic system is like an expression of the Divine Whore in that it links the worlds together by being in relationship with more than one of the other serpents. She rouses the black snake into congress with her when the body is engaged in response and action, and he becomes suppler from her warming presence, but her red roots are fed on the black fruit of him. When he is strong he can exert great power even from a position of perfect stillness, sigils are sent down into his body and swallowed into non-awareness at the high of congress. The red serpent writhes around him and is nourished by his deathly power at the very well of Life.

But the red serpent also craves intercourse with the green and white realms, though the power of the green one cannot exist for long in the human body without the blood converting it to its own nature. The spirits of this realm, the Fair Folk have much the same effect on the spirits closed in red who we call people and animals. Animals of all kinds are attracted to the energy of Faerie but the moment they obtain some of it their first instincts are to convert everything they learn into human form – that is into a logic that will serve the self-interests of their humanity.

Faerie thinking doesn't work like that, so this essential difference, the survival lens red beings have, can cause failures of understanding between these two forms of intelligent sentience. One of the most pressing issues of difference, one that humans seem largely yet to realise, is that whilst they absolutely require the green realm to survive, this entire sentient web of life *can easily continue* to *exist without man, to suckle down his nitrogen and grow vines over her cities.*

Before we even begin to seek the knowledge and conversation of spirits of these realms we must give to them the most important offering any sorcerer can turn up with: our unreserved humility in regards to not privileging our form of intelligence over theirs. Rather than demanding that great ancestors, angels, beasts or faeries communicate with us in our terms, try extending to them a surrender of your Western rational mind as your first sacrifice to them. The part that wants to force their way of thinking through the eye of a needle that is standard human perception! In other words begin from the assumption that every entity or living thing, or collectivity of things, is likely either as smart as you, or smarter, either in the same ways you are or in other ways you can't imagine. Go into these interactions with both the caution and the humility befitting this realisation. Nonetheless stand in your pride and power, for humans too have a holy and rightful place among creation.

Once you get rid of the human-centric way of judging intelligence you will become more open to a wider variety of forms of communication. When before you might have thought you didn't have the Sight, now you might begin to see that you had a narrow idea about what constitutes sight. The old adage about IQ tests being a test to see how well fish do at climbing trees can easily be applied to the world of spirit. Each type does a particular thing that's necessary for life on this planet extremely well, and each magically ignited individual perceives the Otherworld in a specific way right for them. It is possible that you yourself have not yet perfected the carrying out of your role with such clarity as they have. Whatever this spirit contributes, whether it appears closed in red and fur or uses other more ethereal methods to communicate outside our limited perception, it is of a radically equal value.

If you imagine this state of mind will be hard for you to hold onto it might be time to add all the assumptions a Western education gave you to your bundle during this moon of 'rinse and repeat'. Science and mainstream education from childhood teach that our intelligence is the pinnacle point towards which the rest of Nature plays a mere supporting role. To be a good sorcerer you will want to be able to think in the style of as wide a range of different spirits and life forms as possible, to be able to make that switch at will, like a bi- or trilingual person switching between languages. In learning their ways you will get closer to a state of Wholeness, discovering you yourself have your own inner dead men, and women, an inner angel, the opposer, faerie and animal, the uncovering and integrating of these atavistic resurgences is the Holy Graal of some witchcraft practices.

The other radical thing this poetry of coloured serpents is encouraging you to do is to see all things as spirits, even spirits clothed in flesh. Because in an animistic world all spirits have material expressions, whether in the form of a tree or a breath of wind, a certain mountain, lake or mysterious light. The whole world is alive and ensouled and on each smaller breakdown of being lives another smaller discrete set of lives unto itself, none of which, regardless of relative size are any less holy than the others. Such is the animism that underlies the Faerie Faith, with its close connection to witchcraft.

Actualizing these ideas is harder than understanding them. You've probably been at some level resisting both the unity/diversity paradox of things and their fundamental equality for the same reason: because often there is pain involved. It's natural and part of our life impulse to pull back from that which causes pain, but anyone living in a healthy body will have learned a long time ago that some forms of temporary discomfort, such as exercise, are actually good for the body.

It is as though the black serpent powers in Grandmother Fate are telling us that we must learn to be discerning, which, when it comes to the body is really about humility and listening. It doesn't take great wit or learning to know the difference between good pain and bad pain, one need only have learned to pay attention to the wisdom of their flesh. To have learned how to be quiet long enough in our heads, to rip off the voices and opinions of others from our flesh long enough to let the ancestor-wisdom stored in our cells teach us how to be more vigorous.

When you have made an offering to your brothers and sisters among the ranks of the white, red, black and green of your species-centric arrogance you will come out more powerful for it. You will begin to learn the secret tongues of birds and animals, the strange tongue-less chattering the dead make, and pick out the melodies played by the fae on instruments made of dappled light. Strange wordless reciprocations like this will be tendered in the place of your modern hubris, once it falls away. You'll be able to hear them all because you will no longer demand that they speak just like you, or have a face with two eyes and a nose and mouth before you can empathise with them. Things you thought to be voiceless will be heard echoing songs through all creation.

Getting to that place may take many repeats of leaving the

bundle and passing through the other exercises in this book. Sometimes we can't imagine far enough outside the paradigm we've been born into immediately and look back later to smile indulgently at our earlier occult self for thinking they'd left much of anything that first time! Initiation is also a form of radical healing, so when I talk below about what is needed to bring healing to each of the spirit realms, you may find some or all of these suggestions resonate for that realm inside yourself. When we do this work inside we become a catalyst force in the lives of those around us, whether human or spirit, and yet we are always catalyzed by them in turn. This is the gift that keeps on giving which makes the trials and tribulations of sharing our magic with Others radically potent and altogether worth it.

During this moon, go over the work of each moon previous in some large or small way but this time focus on the weaker muscles. If before you worked with the dead who were willing and friendly, now it's time to pick those scabs, to poke the sore spots. Who are your ancestors, both of blood and of the land you live from and on, with whom you are not on good terms? Which among the dead cry out for the resolution of wrongs, for their stories of pain to be told?

Now is the time to sit with your most uncomfortable burdens that the dead bear. Perhaps you must deal with the spirit of a parent who abused you, or perhaps the spirit of an indigenous person your own or somebody else's ancestors displaced or murdered? In some way there is something in everyone's ancestral story that jumps out as the sore spot. You are strong enough now to explore it and attempt whatever reparation can be done, or acted out in a ritual catharsis.

What would you put in your bundle now that you know what you do about yourself from the work of the next ten moons after it? In what ways might shame, the unwillingness to admit to problems or hang-ups one wasn't proud of, stopped you from shedding things you might otherwise have admitted to and let go of some time ago? Perhaps when things go wrong the only move you've learned is to blame someone, yourself or some other and you end up stuck in a self-pity loop?

As correct as you may be in your assessment that someone else was to blame for your situation, it will hardly harm them at all for you to stay where you are, wandering in the loop created for you by an abuser who themselves was stuck in their own hell-knot. When such things are worked through and released the good tends to flow in the direction of the victim anyway, but sometimes also the perpetrator. And this is good news for all of us, because everyone, no matter how victimized no matter how innocent, has been at some point in their history perpetrator as well as victim. So, as somebody's perpetrator (however big or small your transgression against someone, somewhere out there), better outcomes even for perpetrators are in all our best interests …

This being said, better outcomes in some cases might consist of nothing more than oblivion, a condition that is preferable to the hell-loop they are circling in. In other cases you may witness the spirits of individuals who did certain things you don't believe they deserve to be saved from, forgive themselves, reach understanding of why they offended, conquer their hungry ghosts, shed their loop and move on. This may not seem just to you but it's important to remember that there are parts of a person that are not fully responsible for the actions of the shattered ego. When we hold a grievance with someone our fate is knotted to theirs in some way. This doesn't give us a moral imperative to forgive, but it certainly makes it desirable to unknot the connection in some way.

What this means magically is that the person victimized is also more likely to find peace once that link is severed by a motion, whether that is in the direction of oblivion in the heedless guts of the Underworld, or of release and liberation. The better outcome for the innocent party is always more important than remaining bent on revenge at all costs. There are certainly moments where revenge is appropriate, but it's important to realise that the desire for justice can become sentimental rather than practical, and we should always aim for the most practical outcome that upholds our own good. For when we have stopped believing we are worthy of good things, a state of disease is creeping in.

After you have worked through that, a good way to appraise where you're now at is the old occult adage 'to Know, to Will, to Dare, to Keep Silent'. Ideally we want to have a good strong balance of these four characteristics in ourselves before we can move on to become the fully realised sorcerer we were meant to be.

We will apply these virtues to the four colours we've been working with to obtain a deeper understanding of how they manifest.

To Know – Green
To Will – White
To Dare – Red
To Keep Silent – Black

To Know is a fertile power, a growth energy, a stretching out towards objects of knowledge with curiosity. Mystically, we see this reflected in the apple on the Tree of Knowledge coming from the green realm, as well as the herbs in Ceridwen's cauldron. Through lack of this power, people have no interest even in knowing others, no curiosity in finding out about them or the world they live in. Through abundance of the green, we open towards greater understanding as if it were the sun.

To Will is the white serpent of the word that names and stories and reconfigures the patterns of things to create different outcomes. This power is not a blunt-force trauma assertion of force as many imagine; will is a skillful-mean. A lack of it will leave a person at the mercy of the stories of others, unable to direct their own becoming. The presence of will in the sorcerer turns things in their direction through sheer magnetism, like the sun with planets revolving around itself.

To Dare is the plunge into incarnation of the red realm, the courage it takes to extend our awareness into fragile fleshly sensory gloves through which we feel the world. Like the Great Whore who rides the red one, to dare is about deciding to open to the world rather than close in frightened spiritual chastity against the impressions of conflict and agitation. To dare it to blossom in an ecstasy of oneness that leaves no room for fear or Othering.

To Keep Silent is the trick of the black realm, the tongue-less ones ... Can you be silent enough, both with your mouth and your mind, for the faeries to become comfortable with you? Can you be quiet enough that you can hear the dead speak? Can you hold your tongue about what you know, will and dare even when challenged to speak in the town square of what you do in the forest by night? Can you hold your peace even when to do so will convince the populace that you know nothing? Can you hold and not fritter away power? Not losing it via your mouth ... Until you can, there are gifts of the other three powers that you will never have bestowed on you.

The Four Powers of the Mage can also be applied to the four stations of the breath, in-breathing, holding, releasing and holding empty. As you work through those stations during meditation pay especial attention to the one you know you are weakest in, and expose yourself to activities that will strengthen that power in you.

As you go forth into your future experiences with magic, set your intention to become inexorable. Remember, if there is something you want to happen walk towards that experience, turning always towards it and never away from it, until you meet with it upon the road. Be as inexorable as Fate, and as free of sentiment, in this way you will better come to rock the cradle that rules the world. Do not account there to be any such thing as magical failure, only delays in the fruition of your plans. There are instead merely opportunities for trying new strategies that will keep you nimble. If you proceed like this you will meet the destiny you are seeking which by now is also seeking you. You can have any experience you want to when you stop privileging some forms of experience over others.

Conclusions and Gratitude

This spiritual mandate resonates in many ways with the late Andrew D. Chumbley's admonition that sorcerers 'become the Magic which they practise'...

> Thus is the sorcerer, wherever he may wander, become one with the Path of Cain, and the wisdom of the step is declared anew. First, by the stance of Exile as one apart and alone. Second, for the path declared, but also transgressed, its points of oscillation betwixt cure and curse: here the way is bifurcated and become Crooked. Third, for the threefold patterning of Exile, Pilgrimage, and Sojourn that is the bridge linking point-to-point-to-point in crystallisation of knowledge of the Way.
> (Daniel Schulke quoting Andrew Chumbley, Past Magister of Cultus Sabbati)

Rather than making it part of a dry bibliography, I'd like to take this space to reflect on the influence of other writers on this text, and refer you to where you might find some of the wonderful quotes from other thinkers featured here. There are people here in this list of influences that do not like or even appreciate each other's work. Such it is when we meet within the world of man, but it is ever my way to consider the world of both scholar and rogue, genius and trickster and some that might fall between those categories, persons speaking from the head or the heart in research or in poetry, whether they be practising occultists or people of vision and imagination. Some of my work owes direct debts to these people; others are more indirect or form older strata of its foundations.

I have placed them in the order in which they are referenced or drawn on in the text.

David Lewis Williams, *The Mind in the Cave*
The Mabinogion
Rudolph Steiner, *How to Know Higher Worlds*
W.H Auden, *Elegy on the Death of William Butler Yeats*
Mary Oliver, *Wild Geese*
Robin Artisson, *The Flaming Circle*
Fiona Macleod, *The Sin Eater*
Cornelius Agrippa, *Three Books of Occult Philosophy*
Lee Morgan, *Sounds of Infinity* (upcoming from Three Hands Press)
The Tain
Emma Wilby, *The Visions of Isobel Gowdie*
Lee Morgan, *Unless They're Wicked*
David Abram, *The Spell of the Sensuous* and *Forgetting Human*
Sharon Blackie, *The Enchanted Life*
Graham Hancock, *Supernatural*
Andrew Chumbley A. 'The Golden Chain' and 'The Lonely Road' in *Opuscula Magica* Vol. 1 (Three Hand Press 2010) and pretty much everything else he wrote.
Robert Cochrane, *Witch Law in …*
Dr Martin Shaw
Austin Osman Spare
The Secret Commonwealth
Peter Gray, *Apocalyptic Witchcraft*
George Augustus Robinson, *Friendly Mission*
Bayo Akomolafe for *Entangled with the World* who is capable of seeing that there are things that interact with human narratives of how we would like things to happen that make reality more complex and systemic. See specifically:*http://bayoakomolafe.net/project/entangled-with-the-world/*
Martin Coleman *Communing with the Spirits*
Neurolinguistic research about the importance of things being wordable to be found at: http://www.bakadesuyo.com/2017/08/emotionally-intelligent/

Lee Morgan, *Wooing the Echo*
Kahlil Gibran, *The Prophet*
Quotes from Frater A
Schlegel, *Athenaeum Fragments*
Lord Byron, *Fragments*
Dylan Thomas, *Under Milk Wood*

Moon Books

PAGANISM & SHAMANISM

What is Paganism? A religion, a spirituality, an alternative belief system, nature worship? You can find support for all these definitions (and many more) in dictionaries, encyclopaedias, and text books of religion, but subscribe to any one and the truth will evade you. Above all Paganism is a creative pursuit, an encounter with reality, an exploration of meaning and an expression of the soul. Druids, Heathens, Wiccans and others, all contribute their insights and literary riches to the Pagan tradition. Moon Books invites you to begin or to deepen your own encounter, right here, right now.

If you have enjoyed this book, why not tell other readers by posting a review on your preferred book site. Recent bestsellers from Moon Books are:

Journey to the Dark Goddess

How to Return to Your Soul

Jane Meredith

Discover the powerful secrets of the Dark Goddess and transform your depression, grief and pain into healing and integration.

Paperback: 978-1-84694-677-6 ebook: 978-1-78099-223-5

Shamanic Reiki

Expanded Ways of Working with Universal Life Force Energy

Llyn Roberts, Robert Levy

Shamanism and Reiki are each powerful ways of healing; together, their power multiplies. Shamanic Reiki introduces techniques to help healers and Reiki practitioners tap ancient healing wisdom.

Paperback: 978-1-84694-037-8 ebook: 978-1-84694-650-9

Pagan Portals – The Awen Alone

Walking the Path of the Solitary Druid

Joanna van der Hoeven

An introductory guide for the solitary Druid, The Awen Alone will accompany you as you explore, and seek out your own place within the natural world.

Paperback: 978-1-78279-547-6 ebook: 978-1-78279-546-9

A Kitchen Witch's World of Magical Herbs & Plants

Rachel Patterson

A journey into the magical world of herbs and plants, filled with magical uses, folklore, history and practical magic. By popular writer, blogger and kitchen witch, Tansy Firedragon.

Paperback: 978-1-78279-621-3 ebook: 978-1-78279-620-6

Medicine for the Soul

The Complete Book of Shamanic Healing

Ross Heaven

All you will ever need to know about shamanic healing and how to become your own shaman…

Paperback: 978-1-78099-419-2 ebook: 978-1-78099-420-8

Shaman Pathways – The Druid Shaman

Exploring the Celtic Otherworld

Danu Forest

A practical guide to Celtic shamanism with exercises and techniques as well as traditional lore for exploring the Celtic Otherworld.

Paperback: 978-1-78099-615-8 ebook: 978-1-78099-616-5

Traditional Witchcraft for the Woods and Forests

A Witch's Guide to the Woodland with Guided Meditations and Pathworking

Melusine Draco

A Witch's guide to walking alone in the woods, with guided meditations and pathworking.

Paperback: 978-1-84694-803-9 ebook: 978-1-84694-804-6

Wild Earth, Wild Soul

A Manual for an Ecstatic Culture

Bill Pfeiffer

Imagine a nature-based culture so alive and so connected, spreading like wildfire. This book is the first flame…

Paperback: 978-1-78099-187-0 ebook: 978-1-78099-188-7

Naming the Goddess

Trevor Greenfield

Naming the Goddess is written by over eighty adherents and scholars of Goddess and Goddess Spirituality.

Paperback: 978-1-78279-476-9 ebook: 978-1-78279-475-2

Shapeshifting into Higher Consciousness
Heal and Transform Yourself and Our World with Ancient Shamanic and Modern Methods
Llyn Roberts
Ancient and modern methods that you can use every day to transform yourself and make a positive difference in the world.
Paperback: 978-1-84694-843-5 ebook: 978-1-84694-844-2

Readers of ebooks can buy or view any of these bestsellers by clicking on the live link in the title. Most titles are published in paperback and as an ebook. Paperbacks are available in traditional bookshops. Both print and ebook formats are available online.

Find more titles and sign up to our readers' newsletter at http://www.johnhuntpublishing.com/paganism
Follow us on Facebook at https://www.facebook.com/MoonBooks and Twitter at https://twitter.com/MoonBooksJHP